Also by William Irwin Thompson

THE IMAGINATION OF AN INSURRECTION:
    DUBLIN, EASTER 1916
AT THE EDGE OF HISTORY
PASSAGES ABOUT EARTH
EVIL AND WORLD ORDER

DARKNESS AND SCATTERED LIGHT

DARKNESS
AND

William Irwin Thompson

ANCHOR PRESS/DOUBLEDAY
GARDEN CITY, NEW YORK

SCATTERED
LIGHT

Four Talks on the Future

ANCHOR BOOKS
1978

Parts of Chapters One and Two first appeared in *Quest 77* Magazine, copyright © 1977 by Ambassador International Cultural Foundation.

ISBN: 0-385-12877-0
LIBRARY OF CONGRESS CATALOG CARD NUMBER 77-74270

for Beatrice

CONTENTS

ONE.   BEYOND CIVILIZATION OR
        SAVAGERY   10

TWO.   THE METAINDUSTRIAL VILLAGE   54

THREE. THE RETURN OF THE PAST   104

FOUR.   THE FUTURE OF KNOWLEDGE   142

        AFTERWORD   179

        NOTES   185

        ACKNOWLEDGMENTS   191

ONE

BEYOND
CIVILIZATION
OR SAVAGERY

To TAKE A STEP into the future we need to shift our weight to the opposite foot; to think about the future we also need to shift the emphasis to the opposite hemisphere of the brain. The way for a technological society to take a step into the future is to shift the weight of its emphasis from machines to myth.

If we are going to take a step in the transition from civilization to planetization, we will need a map. Each of us carries within, an image of space and time, and this cognitive map tells us who we are, where we come from, and where we are going; but the map also charts a more personal path by which each of us can make his or her own individual way through space and time. The anthropologist A. F. C. Wallace calls this imaging of personal values and cultural forms "the mazeway."[1]

A culture provides an individual with a mapping of time and space, but as the culture goes through a period of change and stressful transformation, the mazeway becomes distorted. The old instructions no longer work and one begins to smash into obstructions he didn't even realize were there. In periods of intense cultural distortion, the mazeway becomes so changed as to be almost obliterated. Then the individual becomes lost, profoundly lost in the most ontological sense of no longer knowing who or what he is, where he comes from, and where he is going. For some this can be a moment of terror, for others, a time of release. In a moment of silence in which the old forms fall away, there comes a new receptivity, a new centering inward, and in an instant there flashes onto the screen of consciousness a new re-*vision*ing of the mazeway. There in the receptive silences of meditation the new possibilities of time and space announce themselves, possibilities that lie beyond the descriptions of the old institutions of the old culture. This is the prophetic moment, the annunciation of a new myth, and the beginning of a new culture.

More often than not, the vision of a new culture may come from an individual's leaving the old civilization behind. In times of overcivilization, or decadence, when the failure of traditional institutions is overwhelmingly apparent, the individual has to leave, to go out into the desert, up into a cave in the mountains, or simply into some remote and distant part of himself. Or the prophetic space can be found in a prison cell. When the individual is taken away from society and locked up within a tiny space, sometimes that space can become an alchemical alembic in which the transformation can occur. In the cases of Malcolm X, Sri Aurobindo, or Baha'u'llah, the prison cell became a way of going out beyond civilization. Abraham was told by God to leave the civilization of Ur behind and go out into the land that God would show him. He had to leave the towers and battlements built by the self-important elite of his time to go out into the desert, for there the walls and towers of man could not obstruct a vision of the cosmic reaches of the stars.

Abraham came out of Ur and went into the desert; and, in many ways, each period of cultural transformation is a touching of the opposites of civilization and wildness, civilization and savagery. Filled with the disenchantment of civilization and its discontents, the disaffected individual longs for other possibilities in the return to wildness, the return to the tribal community, the return to the religious landscape of sand and stars.

And so here we are again. Paradoxically, we are at a moment of technological triumph: the global spread of industrial civilization and the conquest of outer space. All the stone-age tribes have been found and photographed and included in the market system of the world. The economic definition of culture has triumphed, and all the old traditional ways, be they tribal or Christian, seem to be vestiges of a pretechnological era that will be increasingly phased out in the new age. And yet for all the celebrations of progress, we sense a malaise. The economic definition of humanity does not really explain the ultimate meaning of our existence, and the technological landscape cannot tell us who we are, where we come from, and where we are going. The cultural definitions of reality are administered, described, and polished by the elite who run the institutions, but the shine seems glossy and the light seems to bounce off the surface. We begin to wonder how and why the world got into this state and whether there are not other ways in which it all could have gone.

Where did this industrial civilization come from, where is it going, and do we wish to follow it? If we step to the side, we can also look back to see the origins of industrial society in the eighteenth century. In the latter part of the eighteenth century there was the beginning of the distortion of the mazeway, a change in the way people carried the image of time in their minds. In the last quarter of the eighteenth century in Edinburgh there was a group of social theorists called the Scottish primitivists,[2] and their view of time began to question the whole Christian vision of time as a downward movement from the Fall. In this new and radical vision, time did not run downhill but was actually a great ascent from savagery to civilization. They saw the historical curve as moving upward in three great steps: first there was the savagery of the wood-dwellers, then came the period of the agricultural villagers, and finally the achievement of civilization in the creation of the great cities. Fifty years before the work of the Scottish primitivists, Giambattista Vico had published his *The New Science,* in which he had tried to chart "the course the nations ran," but the Scots were no doubt more directly influenced by the contacts with savage peoples that the expanding British Empire was creating. With the travels of James Cook to Australia and Louis, Comte de Bougainville, to Tahiti, Enlightenment Europe could gaze at its mirror-opposite in the image of the savage, noble or ignoble.

In 1770 the Christian vision of the Fall was still the dominant image of time in the culture, and although the new image of progress was being championed in the newly popular learned societies which were springing up everywhere, even in provincial Philadelphia with men like Franklin and Jefferson, the clerical vision of time was still uppermost in people's minds. But the pace of history had begun to speed up, and by 1851 with the construction of the Crystal Palace in London for the Great Exhibition of the industries of the nations, the vision of progress became a public religion, and, perhaps, even a public idolatry.

Since architecture is one way in which a culture makes its collective unconscious visible, the construction of the Crystal Palace in Hyde Park in London is an important moment in the cultural history of the modern world. In the debates in Parliament over the construction of the fairground, a great controversy arose over what to do about the trees that stood in the way of progress. The trees became an unconscious symbol of the natural order of things set against the vaulting ambitions of industrial man. The compromise that was reached was yet another triumph for the ambitious of the new industrial society: the iron and glass structure would be built around the trees. At the unconscious level, industrial civilization was saying: "We have now reached the level of technological progress where culture can surround nature." The Great Exhibition was a celebration of power, the power of culture over nature; nature, like a potted plant, could be miniaturized and contained and put in its proper place.

But the new industrial liberals did not stop there; they went even further to miniaturize Christian civilization. Augustus Welby Pugin designed the Medieval Court for the Exhibition, and what pretended to be only the fashionable nostalgia of the Gothic Revival was really a celebration of power. The Crystal Palace was the new cathedral of the religion of progress; the Gothic art of the cathedrals of Christendom became simply the decorative content in the new and more powerful structure of industrial society. In this foreshadowing of Disneyland, the new capitalists were proclaiming to the new masses that not only did culture surround nature but technology surrounded culture. Those who were the masters of the new technology, therefore, were showing themselves to be *the* new masters. Although Prince Albert initiated the Great Exhibition of 1851, the new initiates of society were not the aristocrats but the Managers.

Prince Albert was hoping in the religion of progress of the times to sublimate military competition in war into peaceful competition in business and international trade. But by the usual movements of opposites in history, industrial society found new ways to modernize warfare. The giant cannons of the house of Krupp were as popular a display in the Crystal Palace as the Gothic reminiscences of Pugin.

But the industrialization of warfare was not the only twist to come out of the Industrial Revolution, for the dance of opposites expressed itself in art as well. Romanticism and industrialization are the double helix of nineteenth-century society. As one side proclaims the new religion of technology and progress, the other celebrates nature and the archaic. As the railroads begin to crisscross the landscape, the poets go out to write poems to the trees. Like an infant pushed out from the womb, the mind had been cast out from nature and was trying to reconstitute its former relationship. So insistent was Wordsworth on trying to put mind back into the landscape that sometimes he would even carve his poem into the very rock where it was composed. The technologists may have been trying to surround nature with culture, but the poets were trying to surround human culture with nature.

Another set of opposed forces in industrial civilization was that of nationalism and global trade. Prince Albert was encouraging the early forms of multinational corporate enterprise. If business could be seen as a missionary force bringing the arts of civilization into all the corners of the globe, then there would be no need for war and conquest, and out of international business could come one global, planetary culture. But the movement of industrialization encouraged its opposite, and the forces of romantic nationalism rose to challenge the triumph of the empire of British industry. By the eighties and nineties all around the world, the small native cultures began to rise up. It was a period of tribes against the Empire. Whether it was the case of Parnell and Home Rule in Ireland, Louis Riel and the métis in Canada, the Ghost Dance in America, or the Mahdi in the Sudan, traditional native culture was being celebrated against the forces of industrial modernization.

Ireland is a fascinating place to study the phenomenon of

the revolt against modernization, for Ireland was one of the first cultures to reject industrial society and to dismember the British Empire in the attempt to create a nation-state. In fighting the battle against the Empire, the Irish developed a peculiar consciousness that has since become symptomatic of most revolutionary movements. The Irish projected their shadow onto the English and claimed that they themselves were all good and that the English were the source of all evil in Ireland. There was no evil in Ireland, the revolutionaries claimed, until the English brought it in after the Norman Conquest. But, as C. G. Jung has warned, if one is not conscious of his internal contradictions, he will project them outward and inflict them upon himself in the form of his fate. The devil kicked out the front door finds an open window in the back. The contradictory personality, caught in the conflict of his own being, shouts a chant of purity and tribal innocence, and then is knocked down by the magnified echoes of his own shouts. Today the Terror continues in Ireland.

The desire for an ancestral tribal purity to stop the encroachment of the modern world is characteristic of many nativistic movements, whether it is the case of the Nazi Germans rejecting decadent France, black Africans rejecting Western civilization, or women rejecting patriarchy with visions of the purity and innocence of the amazonian sisterhood which stood before the march of progress and male civilization.

If one compares Ireland and Germany, he can see two very different responses to the problem of modernization that yet are similar—*in structure, not content*—in that the Irish literary renaissance and German National Socialism are both nativistic movements.[3] In these two cultural movements there is emphasis on tribal archetypal heroes, Siegfried in Germany and Cuchulain in Ireland; and there is emphasis on "das Volk" in peasant arts, crafts, music, and song. Wagner is not Yeats, Germany is not Ireland, and yet these two very different nativistic movements present us with two cultures' differing responses to the problems of mechanization, nationalism, and the relationship between individual and mass consciousness in what Erich Kahler has called the phenomenon of "recollectivization."[4]

Romantic nationalism exercised a great archetypal fascination for the mind of Europe, for it enabled small nations like Ireland, Germany, and Italy, who had been passed up by England and the industrial British Empire, to have visions of becoming the new moral messianic force destined to redeem the world and restore it to its ancestral purity. But what happened in the phenomenon of romantic nationalism is an example of *enantiodromia,* the process in which a movement turns into its exact opposite. The rejection of industrialization in romanticism ended up by becoming the mechanization of romanticism in that blend of nativism and technology, Nazism. The Nazi romantic vision, empowered by the machine, became more pathological and deadly than anything envisioned by the old liberals of Manchester and Birmingham.

History is not a single line but a double helix. The structure of information in our cells is also the archetypal structure of information in the twistings and turnings of the species through time. What starts out in one position ends up in its opposite, and the dream of liberation becomes the nightmare of recollectivization.

If we move from the first Industrial Revolution of the last quarter of the eighteenth century to the second Industrial Revolution of the 1940s, we come to another time when the second stage of the rocket ignites and spaceship earth blasts into a new orbit. 1945, like 1851 before it, became one of those historical moments when the interface between oppo-

sites was most pronounced. Teilhard de Chardin looked at
the atom bomb and noticed that the more the nations tried
to move away from one another to maintain their sover-
eignty, the more they created the necessity to come together
in disarmament talks.[5] In the twisting and turning of the
double helix, conflict created a new kind of peace, the cold
war.

Now what happened in the Second World War was an in-
tensification of the factory system which created the beginning of the end for the factory system. What appeared was a
shift from hardware to information, from coal and iron to oil
and plastics, from bookkeeping to electronics. In the war,
for good and evil, science was wed to government, and the
offspring were cybernetics, atomic energy, and the new postindustrial economy of aerospace companies and university-
industrial research parks. If you consider the fact that in the
Great Exhibition of 1851 the structure of iron and glass surrounded nature and turned Christendom into an artifact in
Pugin's Medieval Court, then you can notice a similar thing
happening in postindustrial Boston. If you look at Boston as
an artifact, you can see that Route 128, the highway which
rings the city and contains all the electronics research firms
spun off from MIT, expresses the new relationships between
government, corporation, and university. The old university
is now surrounded and contained as an artifact within the
new postindustrial structure, just as once the Church was
surrounded and contained as a content within the structure
of industrial society. Harvard and MIT shift from being the
critical wing of society to become a consulting agency for
the government of the new corporate state. In the new university like MIT, the difference between education and
business is blurred. Government, corporation, and university
become one interlocking, bureaucratic corporate system.
What was pioneered by Dr. Vannevar Bush and MIT in the

Second World War has now become the model from the Research Triangle of North Carolina to the Stanford Research Park; and from these centers in America the radiations go out to Canada, Australia, Kuwait, and Iran.

The very giantism of postindustrial society, however, is generating revolt in nativistic movements. As romanticism was to industrial society, so mysticism is to cybernetic society. Whether it is the LSD mysticism of the nativistic leader Ken Kesey, as described in Tom Wolfe's *The Electric Kool-Aid Acid Test*, or the popularity of traditional forms of the esoteric in Yoga, Zen, and Sufism, it is a situation in which the cybernetic shift from hardware to information is generating a shift from churches and clerical real estate to meditation and individual consciousness. As Wordsworth was to the railroads, and D. H. Lawrence was to the factory system, so the gurus are to IBM and NASA. The leaders of the new nativistic movements are the gurus.

But just as all artists are not alike, so all gurus are not alike. Some gurus, such as Ken Kesey, are profoundly conservative and are in reaction against corporate modernization. Other gurus, such as Oscar Ichazo of Arica, are liberals and are really the entrepreneurs of Consciousness Management, Inc. If you look back to the late nineteenth or early twentieth century, you see the archetype of the Entrepreneur, a J. P. Morgan or a John D. Rockefeller. In the founding days of the great corporations, the gigantic structure was the creation of a single visionary, a Westinghouse or a Sloan; but in postindustrial society, the entrepreneur is replaced by the corporate management team. As that happens, the culture begins to compensate and search for another kind of visionary individual who embodies a cosmos, an individual who is figured against the horizon and is not part of the conglomerate structure. The artist was the avatar of romanticism, and the guru is, of course, the avatar of mysticism.

In the September 6, 1976, issue of *Newsweek*, the cover article on the consciousness movement featured a photograph of Muktunanda and Oscar Ichazo seated upon two large thrones on a single dais. In Muktunanda you have the traditional image of the Hindu guru, the guru as Maharaja, whose ashram is a palace; in Oscar Ichazo you have the new image of the guru as Consciousness Management and Company, whose ashram is a corporation. Another and perhaps even more successful example of this type is Werner Erhard and his multimillion dollar corporation, EST. Once again, Erhard, like Ichazo, has gone back to the historical source, in honoring, and, in fact, financing Muktunanda's trip to the United States. Now Muktunanda is not a fraud or a charlatan; he is the real thing, a traditional tantric yogi, but he is limited by his tradition, the Old Age image of the guru as Maharaja. Erhard and Ichazo are trying to absorb him into a new cultural structure. Erhard's relationship to Muktunanda is like Westinghouse's relationship to Nikola Tesla: the entrepreneur buys up the patents from the inventor and then moves into mass distribution. Now you may not like the archetype of the Entrepreneur, in his nineteenth- or twentieth-century guise, but all of us need to remember that each society gets what it deserves.

The guru is a collective representation, a model of individuality in an age of management and general systems. But the way the enantiodromias of history keep flipping back and forth is expressed here as well, for selling consciousness to the individual helps collectivize it. TM moves into the prisons and factories and colleges, EST and Arica into the corporations, and everything comes apart in the shift from civilization to planetization as the factories decentralize and mysticism collectivizes.

These enantiodromias, however, are not only expressed in religious movements; they are expressed as well in the areas of nationalism and the world economy. As national economies become multinational forms of enterprise, you end up with a planetary informational flow in which Holiday Inns, Coca-Cola signs, and airports create one homogeneous culture around the world. The more the world economy spreads, the more nationalism intensifies its attempt to assert itself. In the nineteenth century, it was the revolt of the tribes in the Ghost Dance, the rising of the métis with Louis Riel, or the jihad of the Mahdi in the Sudan. Now we have the revolt of the tribal nations against the forces of modernization, whether in the case of the Irish Republican Army, the Palestinian Liberation Front, or the threatened risings of the Scots, the Welsh, the Basques, the Bretons, and the Serbs. As multinational enterprise begins to satisfy the ambitions of the new global elite, those who are left behind reach out for old symbols to save regionalism in an age of mass consumption.

In the nineteenth century the American Indians attacked the railroads; in the twentieth century the place where tribe and empire confront one another is the airport. On the one hand you have the Holiday Inns and Coca-Cola, as well as the advanced management systems that keep the jets and luggage moving in the proper places; and on the other, the stage for the return of the repressed in the explosion of the irrational in the machine-gunning of tourists, the hijacking, and the bombing. The Manager and the unmanageable Terrorist confront one another, and the monument to progress and technology becomes a stage for the eruption of chaos. As we look at the modern airport it almost seems as if order and terror are the polarities around which the entire postindustrial world economy is organized.

When we look at this modern world system, the postindustrial global economy, it seems as if the beginning of an end is upon us. Immanuel Wallerstein, in his book *The Modern World System*,[6] has described how the world economy came into being with the rise of capitalist agriculture in the sixteenth century. The price of wheat in Poland then began to be part of the relationship of man and nature in England, and the old feudal web of obligations began to dissolve in the new economic definitions of nature, self, and society. Now that we are at the point of maximum expansion of the world economy, it seems as if we are moving from a period of unlimited expansion to consolidation and internal restructuring. The limits on exponential growth imposed by shortages of energy and materials may indeed be telling us that we have come to the end of the modern world system.

The Renaissance witnessed not only the creation of a world economy but the explosion of new religions, and so the contemporary explosion of new religions may be seen as part of a large cultural transformation. As these new and challenging definitions of reality begin to threaten the old world view, we should expect to see a massive attempt on the part of established industrial society to snuff them out. When the Church discovered that tiny and insignificant sects and heresies could really threaten the colossus of the One True Church, it responded to the challenge with the Inquisition, and the seventeenth century witnessed an era of intense religious warfare as the Church tried to abort the birth of the modern world. A. N. Whitehead has described the seventeenth century as "the century of genius," but it was also the century of the Thirty Years' War. Descartes was a genius, but he was also a soldier. In our end is our beginning, and now as we look at the Protestants against the Catholics in Ireland, the Moslems against the Jews in Israel, the Christians against the Moslems in Lebanon, and the Hindus against the Moslems in Bangladesh, it seems as if we have returned to the age of religious warfare. The passion of sect against sect seems to be the antithesis of everything we think of as the nature of the modern world as we travel about in our jumbo jets. When we pick up the newspaper in the morning, what we see is a tissue of contradictions; the very paper itself expresses the utter fragility of the civilization we take for granted in our talk of technological progress.

Looking at these contradictions, I can imagine a scenario for the transition from industrial civilization to a new world order; but rather than sketch the transition positively, I would like to draw it first in negative caricature. Perhaps because I am a historian and not a futurologist, I look back at the tragedies of the past and balance them against any optimistic visions of a "New Age" in which evil will be eliminated. Of course, it is not enough to be a knowledgeable historian: you have to look out of the left eye at tragedy and the right eye at farce, and then see out of the third eye the relationships between the opposites in an ecstasy that literally takes the breath away. Now I don't mean that one should look out at the world in a state of vacuous bliss in which all distinctions are blurred. There may be a single divine sun lighting the tree and the stream, but a distinct tree and a distinct stream are brought together in the distinct life of the sun. In certain kinds of trendy pop mysticism, the devotee blurs the precision of divine creations in an "All is One" incantation; but while the devotees are singing "Hare Krishna" on the streets or passing out lollipop leaflets on the "New Age," the world is busy generating the mirror-opposite in greater and greater acts of terror. The great mystical traditions lead to the illumination, not the elimination, of the mind; and in the clarification of what Joachim of Fiore called the *intellectus spiritualis*, history is seen in the light of myth. If St. John of the Cross found the mystical experience

26

transcending all knowledge and leaving him babbling like a child, he still knew how to return to the illumined mind to write beautiful and brilliant poetry. St. John did not literally babble when he wrote:

> De paz y de piedad
> Era la sciencia perfecta,
> En profunda soledad,
> Entendida vía recta;
> Era cosa tan secreta,
> Que me quedé balbuciendo,
> Toda sciencia transcendiendo.

There needs to be a certain tough-mindedness to the religious vision. If we are too blissfully optimistic, any frustration of our ideals throws us into bitterness and disillusion; if we are too pessimistic, we become unable to do anything at all. Compassion for the suffering of all sentient beings is the vision of the third eye, the vision in which the tragedies and farces of history are seen in a new light.

And so I wish to describe the transition from industrial civilization to what Teilhard de Chardin called "the planetization of mankind" in a tough-minded way. I wish to sketch the transitional scenario in negative terms. Now, one of the most obvious ways of achieving a negative condition is to have things continue just as they are. So let us imagine the first stage of the transition as simply "more of the same." The economic contradictions of inflation and unemployment continue until the bankruptcy of New York becomes the scenario for the nation at large. At that point, the need to stabilize the dollar and put people back to work would encourage Americans to imitate the political patterns of Brazil and Argentina. (In a way, it would be our karma coming back to us.) A president after the manner of Juan Perón could come on the scene to bring Right and Left together in a new political configuration. When Carter went to the 21 Club to have lunch with Henry Ford II of multinational corporate enterprise and Leonard Woodcock of the United Automobile Workers and promised that business would not have to face any new taxation in his first year, he was demonstrating how a marriage of large labor unions and multinational corporations could come about to maintain industrial growth, to maintain high levels of employment, to maintain things as they are.

If industrial society insists upon resisting cultural transformation and insists upon continued economic growth, then it will need energy desperately, and desperate people will do anything to get energy. Conservation and prudence will be swept aside and we will rush ahead with nuclear power and the strip mining of the South and West. Since nuclear power stations will require protection from terrorists, we will move to a condition, even in rural areas, of police surveillance equivalent to that of the airports.

People who are frightened, angry, and out of work will easily give up their civil liberties to a paternalistic state which promises to take good care of them. With pension plans collapsing, the federal government can come in to become the guarantor of the pension funds and the savior of the American middle-class dream of security. But the more people surrender their civil liberties in return for governmental paternalism, the more the terrorists of the extreme Right and Left will seek to disrupt the government. The more terrorism there is, the more the government will seek to protect the population through strong emergency powers. The people will clamor for security and demand to be driven to work in tanks, but the more authoritarian order is imposed, the more revolutionary anarchy will be stimulated. And so the whole culture will spin downward to darkness in a tightening spiral.

With the growth of an authoritarian industrial state of the Brazilian variety, there would also be the growth of all the contradictions of industrial society. With nuclear power, strip mining, and pollution, there would be an increase in environmentally caused diseases. Since the government has already relaxed its regulations on automobile emissions in order to stimulate the industry, and relaxed its air-pollution standards in Long Beach, California, in order to produce the energy needed for industry, it is quite likely that the state will choose to keep people at work rather than worry about long-term problems. Public service announcements on television can inform the people that the government is cracking down on industry, but the propaganda will not be necessary, for the great majority would rather have a new car than clean air. Only the epidemiologists looking at the statistics for the rise of cancer will be able to see the invisible event, but since the hospitals and clinics would be supported by the state, there would be little danger of revolution from the salaried professional class.

Of course, there would be revolts, for we cannot have a movement toward integration at one level without an equal and opposite movement toward disintegration at another. With a movement toward the multinational corporations' vision of global industrial society (the vision of the future of the Trilateral Commission), there would be explosions of movements of nativistic nationalism. Nativistic nationalism may come from the Left, as it did with Allende in Chile, or it may come from the Right, as it did with General Amin in Uganda. Although this nativistic nationalism will be against the multinationals, it will nevertheless be an affirmation of industrial values. The nationalists will simply want to drive out ITT so that they can create their own factories and produce their own pollution. The governments of India and Brazil are good examples of what to expect from nationalism. The very people who create a crisis appeal for emergency powers to deal with the crisis. Ultimately, what comes from the affirmation of industrial civilization by both tyrant and rebel is cultural decay and civilizational collapse.

What is often forgotten in the economic definition of human nature and the econometric description of society is the fact that basic to all our institutions is a moral order and a moral vision. We cannot have even science and technology without a group of scientists and technicians operating with honesty, integrity, and mutual trust. So, as we move toward dictatorships which do not allow dissent, we move toward the collapse of the moral order implicit in even such technocratic areas as science and government.

With moral decay encouraging the growth of incompetent leadership and shortsightedness, the likelihood of nuclear war increases. To fight a conventional war you need good generals and patriotic troops dedicated to the ideals of self-sacrifice. If you cannot trust your generals and are afraid that they might instigate a palace coup, and if the soldiers are simply a pack of undisciplined, pot-smoking civilians, then you know that you cannot maintain a conflict over any length of time in a conventional war. And so in war all dictatorships will be tempted to use nuclear weapons in the hands of small and trusted battalions. If the dictator can hope to achieve a lightning-swift strike over the enemy, then he can dream of increasing his power with the people in a stunning victory. If America is lucky, these nuclear wars will be Chile against Brazil, or Egypt against Iran; if we are unlucky, India against China, or ourselves against the Soviet Union.

If the war is a small strike of, say, Chile against Brazil, then the horror of nuclear war might awaken the world, and the moral vision which brought the United Nations into existence after World War II might renew the vision of a world in which humans beat their swords into plowshares. In the face of the horror of nuclear war, and the prospect of increased nuclear confrontations among all the petty dictators of the world in nations large and small, there could be a resurrection of the old moral order, the vision of all the great universal religions. In a re-visioning of the mazeway, a religious awakening similar to that of the great universal religions in their historical times of crisis, perhaps humanity could finally begin to call into question the very economic definition of man and the econometric description of society upon which industrial civilization is based. On the ashes of the old order, humanity could conceive a much greater and deeper relationship with the planet *in* which it lives than was ever envisioned in the materialist arguments over who ran the shop in capitalism and communism.

This scenario of a transformation in world order is, of course, a more religious version of H. G. Wells's *The Shape of Things to Come*. Wells saw "the freemasonry of science" spreading its "Wings Over the World," but I feel that implicit in science is a moral order which it inherited from the Judeo-Christian tradition, and so I choose to go down to the roots of our civilization in a vision of the sacred, and not merely the scientific. But what you have in my scenario or in Wells's is humanity returning to its senses *after* the dreadful event has happened.

But Heidegger has said that "the dreadful has already happened." If the dreadful has already happened, then, perhaps, so also has the religious, planetary awakening of humanity. All large cultural transformations are invisible; you cannot see the neolithic revolution or the Renaissance in the way in which you can see the bombing of Hiroshima; and so now we cannot see that the religious transformation of the world is already upon us, working to change the culture of earth even before Chile has at it with Brazil.

You will recall that I said that the first stage of the transition was the continuation of things as they are now. In futurologist Herman Kahn's view of industrial civilization, we should go on to achieve a "superindustrial society" of 15 billion people on earth, each allegedly earning $20,000 a year.[7] Kahn is a sort of latter-day prophet of Baal who pronounces oracles which are pleasing to the palace; he and his Hudson Institute give seminars on the future to corporations and charge them $40,000 for the sleight of hand with charts and graphs. Of course, the corporations have it coming to them, but as futurology moves out from the think tank into governmental policy and planning sessions, the joke begins to become serious. With a flourish of an equation, the good doctor Kahn proves that caution and prudence are regressive and that no harm whatsoever can come from the intensive industrialization of the entire planet.

When business becomes your religion as well as your occupation, there is no place to go to get a perspective on things. If the prophet is a futurologist and the poet has become the Nobel Prize winner in economics, then the culture is not that of a civilization but a large corporation. You can put a Picasso behind the receptionist's desk, but that does not mean that art is respected; it simply means that art is good for business. In industrial society the means to an end has become an end in itself, and the maximization of profit has become the driving force of our culture. Culture has become nothing more than an expanding economy. There is no way, the industrialists claim, to impose limits to growth, for stopping would mean loss of millions of jobs; if we truly have compassion for the poor and the homeless, they assert, we must press on to expand the economy. Of course, this is only ideological camouflage, for the industrialists are quite willing to see tolerable levels of unemployment and they do not worry if the presence of their firms in Brazil does not contribute to the distribution of wealth beyond a tiny ruling majority. And so, by pressing onward to Herman Kahn's superindustrial society, our culture becomes overextended and directed toward an even greater civilizational collapse.

And yet nothing seems to be able to stop industrialization. The revolt of romanticism against industrialization did not stop it. Marxism did not stop it. Anarchism did not stop it. The disintegration of the British Empire by tribal nationalism did not stop it. The Beats, the hippies, the New Left radicals of the sixties did not stop it. Like an enormous flood sweeping through a narrow valley, the torrent seems to pick up everything which stands in its way to include it in its own behavior. As you see romantic poet, anarchist, communist, and hippie swept up and floating in the rushing stream, you can see that revolt cannot stop the flood but only lend a little color to the floating debris of history.

Now the mystical movements of the seventies seem about to be swept up in the torrent. Planetary mysticism, the romantic rejection of postindustrial civilization, seems about to be absorbed to become part of the ideological camouflage of planetary management. The French poet Charles Péguy has said, "Tout commence en mystique et finit en politique." Hip management has now moved from Esalen to EST, and even Indira Gandhi has been credited with using Kundalini Yoga to help her save the nation from the perils of an unbridled freedom.

Marx has said that history does repeat itself: the first time is tragedy, the second is farce. I do not think that the American National Socialism which will rise up in an attempt to prolong the death of industrial society will be the openly satanic evil of Nazism, but a farce of parapsychology in politics. In a blend of think-tank management, futurology, encounter groups, parapsychology, EST, Arica, and Scientology, the new super race will not be blue-eyed and blond Aryans but mutants, an evolutionary elite that can operate "on theta levels permanently." The opposition to the mutants can be swept aside as the objection of Neanderthals to Cro-Magnons, and the new parapsychological consultants to the state can move into the schools to administer tests to find other mutants and to teach the less gifted to raise their consciousness "to get it."

The transition from one world order to another which will bring us perilously close to a new kind of fascism is really an initiation experience, a rite of passage. All rites of passage are terrifying, but the images that so frighten us have to be turned inward. In the instructions of *The Tibetan Book of the Dead* the initiate is counseled to realize that the demons he sees are simply the distorted images of beneficent deities. If the initiate can "recall his Buddha-nature" and not fall into a terrifying identification with the demon, then he does not have to be dragged into an incarnation of the hell the demons hold out.

And so the transition from civilization to planetization, from a materialistic industrial society based upon production and consumption to a contemplative culture based upon consciousness and ecological symbiosis, is an initiation experience for the entire human race. The demons we see outside us in the forms of nuclear war, famine, and ecological catastrophes are the terrifying images that accompany the shift from one level of reality to another. Because of the limitations of our egos we cannot realize that we are all part of one single planetary life unless we discover to our horror that we now are threatened by one single planetary death.

There are many ways to describe the process of initiation, but I prefer to see it as a movement in three stages: (1) the illumination of one's darkness, (2) the discovery of the edge of one's sanity, and (3) the defeat or mortification of the ego. In the first stage of illumination, your darkness becomes visible. You discover that, for all the emphasis on ideals and religious values, there is an inner darkness that has been hidden from consciousness. Ironically, the very techniques of yoga that you use to improve yourself are the techniques that bring you to a new consciousness of your shadow. So it is in our civilization. We built up images of ourselves as the carriers of light against the forces of darkness in the Second World War, and then after the war we saw ourselves as the leaders and developers of the world. Now we are forced to see in Viet Nam, in ecological destruction, in economic and social disorder, that we are creatures with an insatiable lust for power. We wish to walk on the moon, to make wheat grow in the desert, to alter the structure of the gene, to control evolution, to build new artificial planets in space. There are no limits to our conscious lust for power, and so everywhere the unconscious is reflecting back to us the images of our wild and primitive exercises of power. What we see terrifies us, for we see the end of a world, an apocalypse; and this *is* an apocalypse, for it is the ending of ourselves and the old world we made for ourselves to be comfortable in.

The old relationship between culture and nature is coming apart, and we are coming apart with nature. It is almost as if consciousness has lurched to the side, out of synchronization with physical evolution itself. Now consciousness is raw, naked, and exposed, and totally unprepared and unknowing of what the relationship between itself and nature should be. Like a nine-month-old fetus on its way out of the womb, it knows there can be no turning back. Cast out from the old nature, consciousness has to allow itself to be mothered at the breast of an even greater nature; it has to release the closing tightness of its grip to experience grace.

But the instant before grace is the moment of terror. It is the moment in initiation in which you experience the breakdown of your whole image of yourself and the reality that goes along with it; it is the moment in which you come to the edge of your sanity and its old normal adjustment to the world. The old image of the ego, whether that of an individual or of a civilization, no longer holds together. You begin yoga thinking that you are going to become better and better, and in a self-congratulatory mood you feel high as you begin to make all the difficult techniques part of your daily life. But as the years go by, you notice that it is the techniques that are taking hold of *you*, and then you discover to your despair that you are not becoming better but worse. The smug self-image of the yogi "on the path" is shattered, and you are forced out of your elation to come to terms with the most basic and fundamental aspects of your own humanity.

When this process happens to a civilization, it is the elite which is humiliated, for the elite is the ego of a civilization. In university and church, government and corporation, the explanatory power of the old tradition collapses, and the conventional morality that individuals used to protect themselves from their demons breaks down. At that point a member of an elite becomes psychologically isolated from his institution and is left defenseless. Every attempt to restore the old becomes only a greater seizure of hysteria, which goes even further to drag the individual out of sanity into madness.

The only hope is to let go and accept your utter helplessness and complete vulnerability. If the initiate feels that he is an accomplished yogi being tested, then the very confidence of his self-image will contribute to an even greater humiliation. If the civilization feels that it is the land of the free and the home of the brave, then it will have its national image dragged through My Lai, Kent State, Watergate, Four Corners, and Black Mesa.

The techniques of Tantra Yoga raise more energy than can be handled by the familiar pieties of the local minister of the social church. The more energy is raised, the more the demons come to feed off the very energy of spiritual transformation. There are real risks and real casualties in Tantra, for there are some who do not make it through but become caught in psychotic states in which they suffer from delusions of religious grandeur.

What happens in the collective situation in which the conventional moral order breaks down is that church and university, government and art, all those institutions that were once pillars of civilization and carriers of the Divine Word, no longer seem to be filled with the holiness, wisdom, and power they once had. Because America has never been defeated in a war, it does not know how to let go and experience its vulnerability. And so it will probably attract to itself a series of ecological catastrophes in which it will be finally forced to surrender its lust for power.

In the case of the individual student of yoga, surrender comes hard. He has been trained for years, preparing body, heart, and mind, but after a while the techniques are usually turned around and used as psychic defenses to protect the personality from surrender.

When you give up, God can give down. When you are totally defeated, you are totally open and receptive. Before, a spiritual ego, a religious self-image which was simply the ego dressed up in a loincloth, protected the personality and came between the individual and God. But in defeat and the complete humiliation of the ego, the individual is completely open to receive grace.

In the wisdom of Christianity, grace can never be earned; the individual Christian is only too keenly aware that nothing he has done or could ever do can make him worthy to receive grace. But when the techniques of yoga are taken out of the context of Hinduism, Buddhism, or Sufism, as they are in America, then the student is subtly led to believe that Kundalini Yoga will produce "an altered state of consciousness" to make a new evolutionary superman. When yoga is taken out of religion and put in the parapsychological laboratory or the human-potential growth center, it is turned into a psychic technology and a source of Faustian inflation for the practitioner. Tantra, or Kundalini, Yoga is not a technique for producing a state of grace; it is a technique for making your darkness visible, for bringing you to the edge of your sanity, and for exposing you to complete and unconditional defeat and surrender.

Our civilization is experiencing the illumination of its darkness; it is beginning to experience the edge of its sanity; it has not yet experienced the complete defeat of its ego. But it will. When? I don't know. I would guess before the century is out.

C. G. Jung has said that a victory for the Self is a defeat for the ego, so perhaps we can assume that the defeat of the civilizational ego is the victory of the new planetary identity, the Selfhood of the earth. What the confrontation of ego and Self is all about is, once again, the interface between opposites. The interface between opposites is the place of transformation. Think of waves on water; where air and water come together, that's where the action is. Where land and sea come together is the turbulent shore where evolution takes a new turn. Or think of the thin film of life, the biosphere, which surrounds the earth and comes between the crust and the upper atmosphere.

The interface between opposites is now conscious and unconscious, culture and nature, civilization and savagery. At this moment we can perhaps best see it as the interface between chaos and creation in the emergence of a new world culture. Think of the pregnant moment of silence in the instant before Creation, when God is envisioning everything that is to be. There is something wild about the totally open potentialities of a universe that is about to be, but has not yet been created. The complete wildness of total potentiality seems almost the annihilation of all possible order; and then the Word is sent forth, the hieroglyph for the universe that is to be with all its systems of order, and out of chaos begin to appear specific limitations. Something like this is going on now in the emergence of a new planetary culture. Now things seem wild and all-inclusive, but as the stable pattern for a world culture emerges, it will grow stronger, more exclusive, and limited. Much that now seems wild, exciting, and open will be lost, but if we are lucky we should have a few centuries of building before the great synthesis freezes into another hierophantic bureaucracy. Now we are a long way from a grand neomedieval synthesis, and as we look out across the contemporary world, it seems very much to be the embodiment of chaos and creation.

Perhaps because I am a cultural historian, I like to see stages to growth, like the three stages of tantric initiation. I think that there are also distinct stages to the contemporary planetary cultural transformation. The stages are part of a sequence in time, but from another point of view they are all going on at the same time, like the voices in a fugue. But for the sake of simplicity, it is easier to separate the voices and consider the four stages of the transformation as separate. The first stage is religious. The second is artistic. The third is scientific and technical. And the fourth is political. The political transformation is the last stage. When everything else is over, then comes the mopping-up action in terms of politics. Most people tend to think that only politics is real and the cultural transformation has finally come into being when it has become political; but from my point of view, the cultural transformation is pretty well over by the time it has become politically implemented.

The first stage of the world-order revolution is the religious stage and is expressed in the visions of such seers as Sri Aurobindo and Teilhard de Chardin. Of course, you could go back as far as the second Isaiah for visions of a new age, but in terms of our specific historical moment, it seems to me clearer to begin with the prophets of the evolutionary transformation of humanity. At the end of the Second World War there was the closing of the era of civilization and the beginning of the era of "planetization," and as one world epoch passed into another, there was a leave-taking of the great Hindu sages: Sri Aurobindo, Ramana Maharishi, and Paramahamsa Yogananda all died within a year or so of one another around 1950. The age of civilization was passing, and with it the age of the guru. We are now in the colorful sunset of the era of the guru, and though it may seem to some that we are being overrun by an influx from Asia, it is simply the explosion of colors at dusk. The New Age is not a Moses on the mountain top or the "Lord of the Universe" before his chosen multitude in the Houston Astrodome; it is not the charismatic individual but the charismatic group, as has been pointed out by David Spangler.[8] After the "Revelation and the Birth of a New Age" with the seers comes the second stage of the transformation, the stage of the artists.

As happened before in medieval or Greek culture, the artists do not create the myth, they express it. Whether it is the composer Karlheinz Stockhausen following Sri Aurobindo, or the novelist Doris Lessing following Sufism, or the poet Gary Snyder following Zen Buddhism, or the architect Paolo Soleri following Teilhard de Chardin, an individual has taken the teachings of a religious teacher and given them a new life in art. In this art a greater part of humanity can begin to sense the imaginative possibilities of a whole new world culture.

The third stage is the emergence of the scientific and technical stewards of the planet—those concerned with how to harmonize human culture within a deeper understanding of the ecology of the earth. These are individuals like Buckminster Fuller, Paul Ehrlich, Dennis and Donnela Meadows, Howard and Eugene Odum, John and Nancy Todd, Aurelio Peccei and the businessmen of the Club of Rome, and the scientists of NASA who have put space technology to the work of planetary resource management. Since such areas of scientific and technical studies seem more real to the general public than religion and art, the third stage attracts an even wider public than the second. With this increasing public attention comes the belated notice of the politicians and the politically ambitious.

Slowly, and very tentatively, the politicians are beginning to think on a planetary level without the usual mind-set of industrial society. When the Prime Minister of Canada, Pierre Trudeau, went to the opening of the New Alchemy Institute in Prince Edward Island in September of 1976, he expressed as well the opening of stage four. When the premier of Prince Edward Island, Alexander Campbell, agreed not to develop nuclear power on the island but to seek out gentler means through sun and wind to create a good life for the islanders with the help of the ecologists, architects, and engineers of the New Alchemy Institute, he too was sounding a new voice in the political forms of world culture. When Governor Edmund Brown, Jr., of California appointed Sim van Der Ryn of the Farallones Institute, an alternative energy and architectural group similar to New Alchemy, to a post as state architect of California, he was recognizing that we are entering a new era in which industrial values cannot be taken for granted. In his presidential campaign Jimmy Carter spoke only of jobs and morality, and thus showed that he was not sensitive to the cultural transformation but was seeking to continue the linear extension of the past. Surrounded by the advisers of the Trilateral Commission, he held a world view shaped by the needs of the multinational corporations; but in his address to the nation on energy in the spring of 1977 he tried to be not merely a manager of industrial society but a leader into a metaindustrial, planetary culture.

Whether or not you agree with Prime Minister Trudeau, Premier Campbell, Governor Brown, or President Carter, the important thing about them politically is that they express the fact that the cultural transformation has now "trickled down" to the politicians, and this is a signal that we are entering the fourth stage. Since it took over a quarter of a century to go from the first stage to the fourth, from the death of Sri Aurobindo to the opening of the New Alchemy Institute in Prince Edward Island, I would imagine that it would take at least the rest of the century to effect a shift in world order in the cultural transformation of global industrial civilization.

The four stages of world transformation express what can be described as the planetary renaissance, and as in the case of the first Renaissance, the new way of looking at the world is coming first from art and scholarship. In Ficino's Academy in Florence, the scholars went back to the Pythagoreanism of the ancient world to create the appropriate intellectual conditions for moving into the modern world. The artists and the scholars came together to envision a new world, not of sin, the Fall, and the necessity to hold to the conservatism of the church, but of new ideas, new energies, new risks, explorations, and adventures. Out of the world of ideas in the fifteenth century came the new economic order of the sixteenth century in the emergence of the world economy in Europe, and out of that world economy came the beginnings of the nation-state system and the rise of modern science in the seventeenth century. And so, if we look at history from a long-term point of view, we have to take myth, ideas, and scholarship very seriously. Dead ideas now support today's dying industrial civilization; new ideas hold the life of a whole culture for the earth.

What these new ideas call for is a re-visioning or a remythologizing of nature, self, and society. In this remythologizing, charisma shifts from technology to contemplative science, from industry to ecology, from factories to communities. Robert Heilbroner has written about "The Decline of Business Civilization," and E. F. Schumacher has said in his lectures that it is the end of the party for industrial society. What these two economists are saying is not that trade and the relationships of human beings through the creation of goods and services are over, but that the celebration of business as the meaning of human culture and the basis for a civilization is over. It would shock all the great civilizations of the world for them to see how we have turned means into ends by making business and industry the sacred in our culture. The fact that postindustrial civilization awards Nobel Prizes to economists speaks volumes on just how much we have lost all sense of perspective and have sunk to venality in even our more ceremonial occasions.

Business and economics will lose their charisma in planetary culture, and in a happier future, the purpose of business will not be seen as the maximization of profit, irrespective of the suffering of the earth and humanity, but simply as an act of service. The businessman will take his place alongside the nurse, the dentist, the postman, the elementary-school teacher.

In the phenomenology of opposites, there is a lovely irony in the coming loss of charisma in business. Business took over the universities in postindustrial society. The university thus lost its charisma and became simply a routine-operational public service corporation, like Consolidated Edison. Now business is being taken out of "the private sector" and is becoming a public service corporation, analogous to the university. There is no such thing as ownership of a university, and as George Cabot Lodge has pointed out in *The New Ideology*, we are reaching the point where we will not be able to speak of the private ownership of a corporation.

We are at the beginning of a new era, and though it looks as if industrial society could go on expanding forever, there are signs that hitherto boom places like California are beginning to experience changes. Business is resisting these changes by simply trying to live the old way by shifting from California to the South, but if the Sun Belt fills up after the fashion of postwar southern California, the twenty-first century will see all the worst nightmares of the ecologists come true in epidemics of environmentally caused diseases which will recall the Black Death of medieval times. The choice is simple: we change our values now to take charisma away from business, or we wait for nature to have the last word. If "the Protestant Ethic and the Spirit of Capitalism" makes its stand in Dixie, and Atlanta and the Research Triangle of North Carolina try to go the way of Los Angeles and Palo Alto, then from the trailer camps of Orlando, Florida, to the tracts of the San Fernando Valley, the South is going to become a wasteland of smog, gas stations, and takeout stands. Fortunately, there is good reason to believe that shortages of capital and energy will save the South from the ravages of the New Atlanteans.

We have already entered the era of limits, and with industrial expansion at its limit, people are beginning to look to other things for the meaning of life. It is time to move on to other visions of the meaning of human culture, and the prophet of this new era was Albert Einstein, who forgot to cash his paycheck from Princeton and ended up using it as a bookmark. In this new era of other forms of growth, workers will be on the boards of directors of their companies, the means of production will be dismantled and returned to regional and ecologically sound forms of production, and the basic unit of production will not be the factory with its appended subdivision of consumptive homes, but the contemplative community like Findhorn in Scotland.[9] New Age communities like Findhorn will become the responsible agents for the production of goods and services in harmony with the basic values of nature. So what we are beginning to see is not the end of business but the end of business civilization.

Since I am speaking about a remythologizing of culture, a re-enchantment to replace the disenchantment that the sociologist Max Weber called the major characteristic of the modern world, I realize that I am going against the major theological trends in culture since the Second World War. European theologians such as Rudolf Bultmann called for a demythologizing of Christianity, and the American theologians who were oriented toward European civilization followed with the "God is dead" movement. But for those of us who came of age in the sixties in California, the world is larger than European civilization. The transmission of the Buddha dharma from the East to the West with the opening of Tibetan and Zen Buddhist monasteries in California is a more important event than all the publications of the demythologizers, for the coming world culture is going to be shaped far more by the contemplative traditions of Buddhism than by the exhausted intellection of European theology.

Since it is not enough to invoke myth without embodying it, I would like to close with a myth and follow the lesson of

Plato to tell "a likely story." I would like to end with the story of Adam's first wife, Lilith. We know of Lilith from the Hebrew Midrash, and as the story goes she was Adam's first wife. Alone in the garden, Adam watched the animals of creation copulating, and asked himself: "Why am I alone? Why can't I have a mate?" This longing of Adam for a mate was the first signal of the break-up of unity into the dialectic of opposites even before the Fall. In longing for sexuality, Adam was moving toward the world of conflict and contradiction; and conflict and contradiction is what Adam found when God granted his wish and created Lilith.

In elation at having a mate, Adam tried to do what he had seen the animals doing, and so he put Lilith on the ground and began to mount her. But Lilith, full of her wildness and instinctive power, was no object to be placed under Adam's power and control, and she demanded to know why he should be on top and she on the bottom. A somewhat inexperienced lover, Adam seems, in effect, to have said, "Shut up and we'll talk about it afterward." This answer did not satisfy Lilith, and so she recited the secret name of God, rose into the air, and went off to cohabit with demons, and lives to this day in the ruins of cities. For the nomadic Hebrews of the desert, Lilith was the voice howling over the mounds of dead and vanished civilizations; she was the female force living in the desolation of male vanities.

Now at the end of a civilizational cycle and at the end of a period of masculine domination, Lilith has returned out of the collective unconscious. What is going on now, especially in the male psyche, is the reconciliation with Lilith. The first response of Man is to be terrified of her, for he sees her as She, the raw, savage bitch-goddess, the destroyer of men, the embodiment of entropy. In the old Babylonian creation myth, the *Enuma Elish*, the great male god, Marduk, tore the Great Mother Goddess, Tiamat, apart to build the great masculine citadel of Babylon. But now as the Goddess draws back the dismembered pieces of her body to regain her ancient life, she is pulling Babylon to pieces. And so men fear the chaos of the feminine and seek always to assert order and control. In the return of Lilith, men fear the end of civilization and the death of all their great cities and industries. The Goddess has come back to take all their toys of civilization away and dance gleefully in the ruins.

But these terrors of the masculine imagination are very much projections. We need in the wisdom of *The Tibetan Book of the Dead* to remember that this terrifying Goddess is really only the malevolent aspect of a beneficent deity; but to remember that, we have to follow the rest of the advice of the book to "recall our Buddha-nature," the consciousness that is greater than any personal ego.

The beneficent aspect of Lilith is that she is the principle of death and release; she comes to release us from the definitions of a single personality or a single civilization, and if we resist her to hold on to the ego of a single incarnation or a single civilization, then her return is terrifying. But if we let go, then we can see that she returns as midwife to our own rebirth. Everything that we think is so important, all the monuments of business civilization and technology, must come tumbling down, for they are external pagan idols which prevent us from seeing the even greater divinity locked up inside ourselves. As Lilith dances in the ruins, there is also a joy of remembering, a joy of other possibilities, a joy of wondering what other nature lay waiting inside her when Adam brushed past it to cast her to the ground and mount her in the roar of a lion.

The reconciliation with Lilith is a reconciliation of the opposites of order and chaos, technology and instinct, civilization and savagery, culture and nature. In male industrial civilization there was an iron wall which separated nature from culture, death from life, irrational from rational, male from female; but in the metaindustrial culture of the future there is only a light permeable membrane between them. And since architecture is an expression of the collective unconscious, this shift from wall to membrane has already begun to express itself in the new symbiotic architecture in which solar membranes and cloud gels surround the "bioshelters" of Day Charoudhi and Sean Wellesley-Miller. At an archetypal level, these new forms of symbiotic architecture should be seen as appearances of the feminine principle, a movement away from the dominant rectilinearity and technology of the Bauhaus international style to curve, cloud, and membrane. The movement is one from technological control and avoidance of mother nature to working with natural forces at a subtle level. In the terms of the New Alchemist John Todd, it is a movement from hardware to information.

In this shift from hardware to information there is developing a new relationship between culture and nature in the emergence of a new instinctive technology. Always before, our efforts were to replace instinct with technology, to replace nature with culture. Whenever we were threatened by the expressions of a wild and uncontrollable nature, we would send in the cavalry, the marines, the antibiotics. Now we are beginning to realize that there are other ways to live; we are beginning to see that health is not a collection of quick fixes for a catalogue of diseases but an integral way of life.[10]

As we shift from hardware to information in ecology, architecture, and medicine, we shift from viewing the world as arranged in categories protected by iron walls to seeing it as a living organism in which permeable membranes allow information to pass through while still respecting the integrity of the cell. This transformation of our way of looking at the world expresses itself everywhere, for just as there is now a new membrane between nature and culture, so is there now a new membrane between the ego and the soul, or daimon. (I will go into this in more detail in the last talk, on the future of knowledge and the return of hieroglyphic thinking.) Once we were separated and encapsulated in our egos; we either had no sense of our souls or connected with them only in a few seconds of religious experience. There was an iron wall that completely shut off the ego from the daimon. But now, in the return of mysticism to popular culture, the wall is dissolving. The ego is not being annihilated, for it exists for a reason, but in a healthier affirmation of the limited use of the ego by a soul, the relationship between ego and soul is becoming symbiotic. Techniques which seek ego annihilation, such as those of Arica, are simply the mirror-opposite of the industrial modes of thought which shut out the soul to emphasize only the ego. One extreme always generates its opposite extreme, but a healthy balance, or Unity of Being, is in neither position. In the wisdom of esoteric Christianity, there is a purpose, a sacred purpose for the mystery of incarnation. When the ego is *figured* against the *ground* of the soul, there exists only a light-permeable membrane between them; across this membrane information can pass, and the ego can begin to know through the higher consciousness of the intuition.

But just as there is a light-permeable membrane between ego and daimon, so is there one between ego and society. The nineteenth century saw the rise of the notion of the unconscious, and the emergence of a new experience of the collective unconscious in the political recollectivizations of romantic nationalism. What I think we are beginning to see now is the emergence of a collective consciousness. In the mystical cults of ego annihilation, the individual is wiped out in an ecstatic adulation of the guru. In mass cults, the individual is wiped out in ecstatic adulation of the state. Both cases are unhealthy and pathological. In a healthier collective consciousness, the individual is aware of the presence of the group-mind, but his own integrity is not crushed by it. It is one thing to be forced to sing the company song in the morning, and quite another to sing Handel in a chorus; in one case, individuality is eliminated, in the other, it is uplifted.

The rise of a collective consciousness will also give rise to visions of terror and recollectivization. Men will fear the return of the beehive and Queen Bee, and in nightmares they will dream of the return of Lilith. Women, once excluded from power, will seek to extend the life of the dying culture of machismo by becoming industrial amazons. Labor unions will melt into the corporations as the corporations promise job security for life; the corporations will melt into the State, as the State promises contracts for life, and the State will become all in all: union, corporation, and university in one.

To avoid this shadow form of the emergence of a collective consciousness, people will strive to build fortresses of self-sufficiency. For the Right wing, these fortresses will be bomb-shelter nuclear-family homes, with food and water stored up against disaster, and with plenty of guns and ammunition to drive off roaming bands of looters. For the hippies, the vision will be one of a totally self-sufficient commune, where the tribal family will have its *own* food growing, its *own* energy from the sun and the wind, and its *own* laws. But whether your hero is Ronald Reagan or the hippie leader of "The Farm," Steve Gaskin, your dream of surviving while everyone gets the apocalypse he deserves is a dream of the ego trying to build castles for itself.

There is no such thing as self-sufficiency. As A. N. Whitehead pointed out even before the age of ecology, everything "prehends" everything else. The earth is a single living cell and we are organelles within it.[11] The lead from the exhausts of the cars on the freeways in Los Angeles circulates through the currents of the atmosphere and falls in heavy concentrations in the Arctic, where it is absorbed in the food chains of the Eskimo.

As we begin to realize from our new images of biology that we are organelles within a single cell, our images of society will change from the conventional vision of competition and aggression to one of co-operation and symbiosis. And just as the biology of Darwin had political repercussions, so will this new biology. We will begin to become sensitive to the emergence of the collective consciousness of the human race. The shadow side of this will be the danger of political collectivization in the colossal institutions of a desperate and dying industrial system; the positive aspect is the cultural evolution to a metaindustrial society and a higher level of spiritual consciousness. At the moment, the emergence of the collective consciousness is polarized around the opposites of China and America, for these two countries are more than nations; they are archetypes. China expresses the power of the group, and as one large racial unit, sees the collectivity of the *species* as the evolving unit. America expresses the power of the individual. The individual carries the DNA of the race; the individual is the basic unit of evolution, and all evolution works to bring into being new levels of personhood and higher consciousness. The shadow side of American individuality is fragmented communities and disrupted ecologies; the shadow side of Chinese communism is totalitarian suppression of the evolution of consciousness through the higher Self. America and China are opposites now, but in the attraction of opposites, each is fascinated with the other. In the next quarter century, I think we will see a marriage of these opposites, bringing communalism to America and individuality to China. If we are lucky and the meeting of the opposites is a marriage and not a war, then we should begin to see the evolution of a new personhood figured against the ground of a new collective consciousness. The reconciliation of these opposites is all part of the myth of the reconciliation with Lilith.

The wild first wife of Adam is pure instinct. The second wife, Eve, is passion and emotion. Lucifer is the god of selfishness, who tempts Eve's passions with an appeal to her selfishness. In eating the apple, Eve takes in the food and makes it part of her body to empower herself. Christ is Lucifer's opposite, who gives of his own body to empower the communion. As Lilith and Lucifer surface out of the collective unconscious, the drama of human evolution turns on the spiral to go back to a point as critical as the Fall, and we tremble again with temptations that offer technologies in which we will become as gods, and fear another Fall that will drop the human race into darkness and oblivion. But if we again take our counsel from *The Tibetan Book of the Dead* to realize that Lilith and Lucifer are the malevolent aspects of beneficent deities, then we can recall our Buddha-nature to see that Lilith and Lucifer are simply what the old Adam conceived them to be. As we draw back our projections into ourselves in contemplation, the world outside changes as if we were pulling aside the curtains to look out on a wholly new landscape to see how God has been making love with us out of time.

TWO

THE
METAINDUSTRIAL
VILLAGE

I CONCENTRATED BEFORE on a negative scenario for the transition from the present international system to a new world order. Now I would like to focus on a more positive way in which America can take on a new life in its role as the charismatic archetype of prosperous and powerful nationhood. Since all the world is trying to go the way of post-industrial civilization, all the world is imitating us, and if we create Los Angeles, then the Iranians or the Australians will try to have superhighways, smog, and traffic jams too. And so the way to change world culture is to come home to work for a transformation of the archetype of industrialization itself.

Human nature being what it is, it is fair to say that change comes from snobbery and elitism; what a respected section of the population has, others soon want too. If a farmer feels that his father was a hick and that businessmen constitute the elite, then he will work hard to become an agribusinessman and begin to buy chemical fertilizers, computers, and huge machines. He will pay for oil-burning trucks to come in and haul his manure away and replace it with the products of Shell and Monsanto; he will milk his cows by machine and inseminate them artificially in factorylike barns. There is no good reason for this; in fact, there are some very good reasons why he should not. But since his pappy was a hick and was looked down upon by all the city slickers, he wants to stand as tall as the other guy, and so he becomes an industrialist to grow his potatoes with oil and dry his corn with our dwindling reserves of natural gas.

To change all this, we have to get down to the roots of the whole way in which people think. "Reality" has very little to do with economics, but economics has a great deal to do with mythologies. The images and archetypes that people carry in their heads shape their reality. I would stand Marx on his head to say that it is not the means of production, or the technology, that shapes human consciousness, but human consciousness that shapes the technology and the means of production. But, of course, it is not a case of "either/or" but "both/and." Consciousness affects technology, and the feedback of technology on consciousness changes consciousness, and that is what culture is all about. In our industrial culture, people *think* that only technology matters, and they cannot see that their minds have been captured by the mythology of the machine. Since it was an elite, first British then American, which generated the mythology of industrialization, we need to see that if we are going to transform postindustrial society, we will need a new elite with a new mythology.

The mythology of the country hick and the city slicker is a very ancient one; in fact, it is a way of experiencing human culture that goes all the way back to the urban revolution in Mesopotamia. If you go back to the rise of cities in ancient Sumer and begin to consider the *idea* of civilization, of *civitas*, then you can see a dramatic shift in the whole cultural imaging of time and space, a whole transformation of the "mazeway."

In hunting and gathering societies, people live in what

anthropologists call "the seasonal round." There is a delicate kind of adjustment of the tribal band to nature; the band moves through space with the flow of time: when the salmon are running, it comes to the particular stream, when the nuts are ripe in another place, it is there at that time; when the wild grasses are ready for gathering, it moves on again. The band circulates through space in the rhythm of the seasons, returning to winter camp and summer camp with each year. Time is a round, the eternal round, the eternal feminine. The circle is not broken into a line; the tribe does not stay in one place to alter nature to suit the needs of the human settlement.

So the urban revolution is a profound revolution in consciousness; it is a profound revolution in the relationship of culture to nature. In domesticating plants and animals, managing the flow of rivers, and restructuring itself to stay in one place for all time, society changes from a movement around the circumference of the seasonal round to the creation of a line, the radius which marks out the distance from the center to the periphery.

The basic structure of civilization is a dialectical tension between center and periphery. In terms of the energy grid that supports a nucleated settlement, the resources come from the periphery and are controlled at the center. Whether the energy is the water coming from upstream in the Nile or Tigris, or the oil coming from Alaska, the resources are at the periphery, where the hicks are, and are controlled at the center, where the elite are. The elite at the center have the particular informational mysteries through which resources can be controlled, manipulated, and managed, for they have writing. Whether it is the cuneiform on stone tablets which marks the amount of grain contributed by the farmers to the temple granary, or the geometrical forms of land-surveying which mark out the area inundated by the Nile, the mystery of writing enables the elite to separate themselves from the tribal illiterate masses.

The way in which the elite express themselves is through the city. The city is literally civilization; the city is the control of the periphery by the center. Now what makes the city possible is its ability to store enormous amounts of personally unintegrated information. Tribal human beings have enormous memories; the women are meticulous botanists in their lives as gatherers, and the men, zoologists and geographers. A tribal bard can recite from memory poems as long as the *Iliad*. But in tribal, oral culture, the knowledge is integrated in the folkways of life: there are no "facts," there are only experiences and events. It is when we come to write on stone tablets and have cadres of scribes that we get facts; then we have so many jars of grain, so many flasks of wine. The knowledge is disconnected from the mind and body and is stored in the alien spaces of an institution.

Writing creates another dialectic of center and periphery, for the sensations at the periphery of the body are brought to the center and constellated there in an ego. As civilization moves toward the collectivization of tribes into the city, there is a compensatory and opposite thrust toward the creation of a new personhood, a new ego. Carlos Castaneda's Don Juan has said that the civilized man looks at the world with his eyes and interprets what he "sees" through abstractions, but the sorcerer knows how to perceive with his entire body; he can step out of the habitual description of reality to "stop the world" and "see." And so for precivilized humans there is a diffused peripheral perception in which the skin isn't such a hard edge, and the body blends into the larger organism of the environment. There is almost a fetal, amniotic continuity, the oceanic oneness which Freud talks about, between the hunter or gatherer and his or her surrounding world of animals and plants and spirits. It is a state of being which civilized human beings have to work to recover through years of removing the obstructions of the civilized mind to perceive and be in the world through the empty fullness of Zen meditation.

Thus when sentience and the body's own perception of itself are taken from the periphery and organized at the center in an ego, a process takes place which is similar to that going on in the body politic. The ego is to the body what the elite is to the city. Consciousness is taken from the periphery to the center and there, through a system of abstractions and a control of information, a new entity is constellated, and you get the individual ego which can feel its own separateness from the tribal community. Mythologically, this shift is expressed in a movement away from the Great Mother Goddess of the Neolithic to the new masculine gods who organize the world. In the Sumerian poem "Enki and the World Order" we see the old agricultural Great Goddess being replaced by the new dynamic male gods. The god of the neolithic is the Great Mother, but the god of the urban revolution is male, and in the Babylonian creation myth, as we have seen, it is Marduk who tears apart the body of the Great Mother Goddess to build the new world order which culminates in the construction of the great city of Babylon.

The Sumerian and Babylonian myths enable us to see into the process of change in the urban revolution, to see the psychological dimensions of the appearance of writing, government, and warfare. And what we see there is a double helix of increasing collectivization and increasing individuation, a process of increasing personhood. Over the past five millennia since the urban revolution, we have seen many changes, but we have not seen a reversal of this process of increasing individuation. Once personhood was celebrated in the form of the pharaoh or king; then it was extended down to the aristocracy and the military class, and then finally down to the merchant class. By the time of Rome, the extension of personhood had reached the point where a citizen of the Roman Empire did not have to be rich. When St. Paul is taken prisoner, his whole treatment changes as he informs his guards that he is a Roman citizen.

What we see in this relationship between civilization and personhood is an example of Teilhard de Chardin's thesis that "collectivization leads to hyperpersonalization." So, once again, we can see that the idea of civilization is based upon dialectical thinking, of center and periphery, city and citizen. But when you are thinking dialectically, you are basically talking about a system of tension, a system of conflict. The manner in which Unity is expressed is in the conflict of opposites—good and evil, light and dark, male and female, country and city. In the Old Testament we see this conflict expressed in the antagonism between the tent and the temple. The people at the periphery are the Habiru, the dusty nomads of Father Abraham; they are the wise people who have seen cities come and go. The people at the center are the people of Pharaoh. But when the Hebrews leave Egypt, they build themselves a little Egypt and King Solomon becomes another pharaoh. Solomon, to celebrate Israel's new-found power, wishes to build a temple; he wants people turning toward *his* temple when they pray; he does not want to see them praying on rugs on the desert sand or in the tents of the patriarchs of the great tribes. And so he petitions Jahweh to enter the Canaanitic temple he has built, but Jahweh is not certain about the value of temples and cities, and He says, "In as much as I have always been a dweller within tents," and expresses concern for the New Israel. But King Solomon promises to keep Jahweh's laws, and so a covenant is made. Flushed with his success, Solomon tells the people that they must now turn toward this, his temple when they pray. The state has grown up as the middleman between tribal man and his God. The days of Father Abraham are over, for the Hebrews have achieved civilization and its discontents, and neither the warnings of Samuel nor Jahweh himself could save them. By the end of his life, Solomon is lighting candles to Ishtar and forgetting the covenant with Jahweh, and thus revealing that the construction of the temple was not to please the God of Abraham, Isaac, and Jacob, but for the good of the state. The temple was built by Canaanitic specialists, and, therefore, had to express civilized notions of worship. From the tower of Babel to the temple of Solomon, cities and their temples mean class stratification, alienation, the accumulation of wealth, and all the familiar contradictions of civilization.

The Old Testament is more profound than any recent sociology in treating the conflict between the city and the country, the center and the periphery. In the desert you can put the pretensions of man far behind and, in a landscape of sand and stars, set the scale right to remember the original covenant with Abraham. Whether it is Moses or Mohammed, the vision comes in the desert, and then the prophet returns to conquer the city.

The landscape of the city is a celebration of power; the monuments celebrate kings, the stelae celebrate the conquest of armies. The city breaks up the tribal community and makes the rise of an individual ego possible, and then the ego runs wild and tries to reconnect itself through the accumulation of wealth and power.

What you have in the conflict between the desert and the city is the conflict between the conservative and the liberal vision of values and time. For the conservative, tribal human being, all value rests at the dawn of time, with the ancient ones, with Father Abraham and the original covenant with Jahweh. But the progressive liberal says, "No, we were slaves under Pharaoh, but now we are rich and can buy our own slaves and build our own great temples." In the liberal vision value is seen in the present, not the past. The new times require new laws and new customs—standing armies, taxation, temples, world trade. The liberal vision is a linear one of progress, development, and the increase in the Gross National Product. The conservative vision is of the eternal round, the circle which is full round and filled. The linear aspect of the liberal vision is much more flattened out, for it is basically the vision of management: time can be managed, space can be managed, and even, with appropriate temple rites, God can be managed. Thus the conflict between desert and city, conservative and liberal, is the conflict between the prophet and the priest. It is the prophet Amos who declaims against temples: "I despise your feast days, and I will not smell in your solemn assemblies."

The prophet is chosen by God, but the priest is chosen by man; one comes out of the desert having endured some overwhelming shamanistic experience, the other, out of an institution, having experienced "the best" training "the best" people can give him. All through the Bible we see the conflict between prophet and priest; the crucifixion of Jesus by Caiaphas is the final culmination of the mythic pattern.

Now as we look back over this dialectical pattern of prophet and priest, periphery and center, we can see that civilization is, literally, what goes on in cities: *civitas*. The city is where it's at. It's where the palace is, where the temple is, where the marketplace is. It's where the power is for the aspiring elite and the jobs are for the indigent masses. In bringing together top and bottom, you create the pyramid of civilized society.

In contrasting the desert of the tribal nomadic community, or the band of hunters and gatherers, with the city-state, I have passed over another kind of community which may help us to find a way out of the conflict between tribe and city, and that community is the neolithic village, or its more recent form, the preindustrial village. If you compare the preindustrial village with the city, you see a totally different arrangement of time and space in consciousness. The mazeway of village life is neither the desert of the solitary prophet nor the labyrinth of the urban masses. Even as late as the eighteenth century in England, the preindustrial village provided the individual with a different way of moving through time and space, a different way of knowing his basic identity.

Identity is based upon internalized images of time and space. The image of time comes from the family name; the family name is a piece of time. So if your name is Thompson, it means son of Tom, and is a Danish form of the more ancient Gaelic name MacTavish. The family name tells you not only who your father is, but who your people are, where you come from, and where you can expect to go. The family name becomes the way in which you can carry the burden of generational time: so and so begat so and so. In a traditional culture, if you can't recite your lineage, you are disconnected, ignorant, and utterly lost. In ancient Ireland when bards would contest with one another, they would recite their lineages, and the one who could go on for the longest time won, for he had the longest memory and therefore could connect himself to time and space, could connect his society to the universe. The shallow and ignorant person, by contrast, doesn't know who he is, where he comes from, and where he is going.

Now just as the image of time is carried in one's family name, the image of space is carried in one's soil. There exists a personal relationship to the landscape, for preindustrial man will more often than not live and die in the same place. In recent medical studies of longevity around the world, the researchers have found that what all the aged people have in common is that they are not mobile; they live and die in the same place; they are not constantly uprooted and transplanted. And so preindustrial man has a magical affinity with the landscape; subtle etheric forces nourish him. We have lost this knowledge, but it is our own fault, for poets like Wordsworth and D. H. Lawrence did their best to remind us.

The soil is the ground of your being; and so between the earth and your family name, soil and blood, you know how you are connected to the basic ontological scheme of your culture *in* nature. But the difficulty with this lovely, nestling, comforting sense of community is, of course, that it is also a prison. From another point of view, the squire and the parson are the jailkeepers of the preindustrial village. They know who you are, what your class situation is, and, therefore, what your expectations can and cannot be. Village life is close and intimate; the moral order is close and strict, and so everyone can keep an eye on you.

The comfortable body of community is also a body of restraint. In a sense, you can only have community by giving up certain amounts of personal freedom. The ties that bind may not be iron chains, but they can tie you up just as effectively. And so, once again, we encounter a paradox: community equals constraint; freedom equals alienation. Freedom means the freedom for some people to become lost, just as it means the freedom for some people to find themselves in a new space and a new time.

Now one of the dominant myths of industrial society, a myth which created a new mazeway of time and space, is the myth of freedom. The charismatic myth which industrialization held out to the traditional world was, and still is, the myth of freedom. Suddenly the villager can be free of blood and soil, can leave it all behind him to go to the city and create a whole new identity. The city offers a whole new constellation of space; you have Dickens's London or Dreiser's Chicago. You leave the farm behind you; you leave the country hicks behind you, and you go to the city "to make it." The city offers a new image of time. You are finally free of the family name. If you are an immigrant to the New World, you can throw away your unpronounceable name to work to become a rich man. In "making it," you are, of course, simply remaking yourself in ways that were impossible in the shtetls of Russia or the potato fields of Ireland.

The charismatic myth of freedom in industrial society is the myth of "rags to riches." You see it everywhere expressed in the popular mythologies of literature, for it is the basic myth of the expanding middle classes. You see it in *Moll Flanders, Great Expectations,* the books of Horatio Alger. The country holds out what Karl Marx at work in London in the British Museum would call "the idiocy of rural life." And so the myth all the way back to Shakespeare is to leave Stratford-upon-Avon, make it in London, and then return in power to lord it over the hicks by buying the biggest house in town, regaining the old family crest, and becoming a squire in one's own right.

What the industrial myth of freedom expresses is the tacit formula: "You are what you own." The earth and your family name can be ignored; it's your personal patterns of consumption that tell people all about you. And so, *if you are what you own, the more you own, the more you are.* Consumption becomes intimately linked to the new mazeway, for the manner in which you make your way through space and time is through buying things. This is one reason why in places like Watts in Los Angeles, having a certain kind of car or a color television set is much more important than renting a nice house or apartment. The television set and the car give you freedom and mobility: the freedom of informational flow with a window on the world; the freedom where no one can ever again lock you into the soil behind a mule in Tennessee; the freedom to step into your big car, get on the freeway, and roar across the landscape as if it all belonged to you. Cars and television sets are not simply purchases: they are profound creations of personhood; individual identity is all tied up in them. And just as blood and soil were once the ties that bound, so now the purchases, especially the time-payment purchases, become the ties that bind and lock the individual into a whole new loss of freedom.

As everything moves to a brilliant sunset before it vanishes, the culture of consumption has now reached its most hysterical level of intensity. Millions of people all over the world are fleeing the idiocy of rural life to crowd into Calcutta, Bombay, Hong Kong, Teheran, Caracas, and London. The peasants are throwing away their handmade tortillas, pita, and papadams, and demanding Ritz crackers and Coca-Cola. And in the country which has supplied them not only with the crackers and Coke but with the consciousness which makes them want to industrialize, we have set an example of a consumer society in which only 6 per cent of the world's population consumes 30 per cent of the world's resources and produces an equivalent level of pollution. We are the charismatic archetype all others follow. And so if we get rich by turning our forests into Kleenex, the Brazilians scream that they want to turn the Amazon into a parking lot.

Ultimately, the world of consumerism ends up by consuming itself. Rural farm and ranch lands are destroyed in strip mining so that the roulette wheels can keep turning in Las Vegas and the TVs keep shining in Hollywood. Resources are depleted in making shoddy goods with built-in obsolescence so that high levels of employment can be maintained. Industrial growth, the industrial managers contend, must be maintained; and so the maintenance of industrial growth leads to the end of industrial civilization. Civilization, at its maximum point of expansion, reaches the breaking point, the place where "the center cannot hold, mere anarchy is loosed upon the world." The relationship between center and periphery, the very dialectic of civilization, breaks down.

We have reached the point of the limit of civilization and urbanization. In America 2 per cent of the population feeds the other 98 per cent; 80 per cent of the population lives on less than 10 per cent of the available land. The postwar development of California expresses the nature of this culture and all its contradictions. Once upon a time a great king in India built a great and important city, and after the city was built, the water table dried up, and the city had to be abandoned. Now Fatehpur Sikri is a glorious and romantic ruin. There are other ruins of cities that had to be abandoned, like the ceremonial centers of the Maya in Central America; and so you cannot help but wonder about the viability of California. The entire colossal pyramid of postindustrial civilization is resting upon its point, and that most narrow of foundations is fossil fuel. Oil is used to bring up the water from the earth or carry it from the distant mountains; petrochemicals are used to fertilize the fields and kill the insects; fuel is used to plant and harvest with machines; fuel is used to transport food to the market, to wrap it in cellophane, to refrigerate it in trucks, stores, and homes. Old varieties of plants are passing into extinction, and now only the seeds of the new hybrids remain, seeds of varieties that require massive amounts of insecticide to survive, or varieties that have to be dried artificially with natural gas before storage. A slight flick of the little finger of Mother Nature, a drought for a mere five years in a row combined with an intense cold spell during the winters, and hundreds of millions of people could die of starvation around the world. As happened before, in the second millennium B.C., there would be a great *Völkerwanderung* that would make the Dust Bowl of the thirties seem insignificant. The great cloverleaf freeways of Los Angeles would be swept clean by sand and desert winds to become an enigmatic sphinx for the remaining generations of the future to decipher.

Industrial civilization was built on coal; postindustrial civilization is built on oil, and so the battle over the control of oil expresses the increasing tension between the periphery and the center. The center can no longer control the periphery: the Scots do not want their oil controlled in London, the Alaskans do not want their oil controlled in New York, and the Arabs do not want their oil controlled by the Seven Sisters oil companies. Nationalism returns to challenge multinational enterprise, and Scotland and Alaska begin to wonder if they cannot become independent nations like Kuwait and Libya.

But the problem is not simply the availability of oil, but the cost in getting it. Since it takes energy to produce energy, there is a law of diminishing returns, and the net energy gained, as Howard Odum has pointed out,[1] is not always a gain at all. The American oil companies decided to avoid the expensive extraction of American resources to make a quicker buck with Middle Eastern oil; now because of inflation, the cost of making America oil-independent has increased enormously. Our response is to trade armaments for oil with Iran, and so the vicious circle tightens the noose around postindustrial civilization as we contribute to the instability of the nation-state system by selling billions of dollars in arms to the Shah and the sheiks.

The problems are compounded when you stop to think that the flow of oil and currencies is not simply a matter of resources but of informational flow. Up to the nineteenth century, a person could be educated by having at his fingertips a few hundred books. Now there are forty thousand books published a year in the United States alone, and over a million scientific papers published annually in the world at large. The ability of elites to organize information at the center is breaking down, and the power of their old descriptions of reality are weakening. Since no one can relate to the overload of information, individuals have had to specialize, but specialization has disconnected the elite from the civilizational system. The technocratic specialists have tried to become the elite of postindustrial civilization, to do for our society what the elites of parliament, church, and university once did for traditional society, but their tunnel vision has created the culture now consumately expressed in California. Technocrats are leaders, leaders directing the stampede over the cliff. To step back from the herd to get a sense of the entire landscape, you need to think in ways that are not fostered by our schools.

In the age of literacy, when literature set the standard for education, an individual was expected to be able to express himself with a sense for prose style. E. B. White was a popular model of the man of letters, and thousands of university students had to commit the little red book of Strunk and White to memory; then came the electronic culture of the sixties, and freshman English was dropped and replaced with more "relevant" courses on political and sexual liberation. In the new electronic oral culture of the media, the letter was replaced by the phone call, the novel by the film, and history by televised news documentaries. The cumulative effect of this shift is expressed in the fact that literacy levels have declined so much that publishers must now turn out college textbooks written at a tenth-grade level.

The reason for the decline in literacy is not hard to uncover, for no one bothers to teach students in high school and college how to write. The high school teachers go home to watch *Kojak*, not to grade themes, and so the students are given multiple-choice questions on machine-scored tests. The popular teacher is not the antique grammarian but a Merv Griffin who runs class discussions after the fashion of a talk show. When the student enters college, he finds that his professors are more committed to their highly specialized areas of graduate research than to teaching the banalities of general education, and so he is pushed into the tunnels of specialization as quickly as possible. The student burrows into his hole, but takes his portable television set down with him so that he can maintain a sense of perspective on society at large by continuing his membership in the only generalized culture he knows.

What the media have done is to create a new electronic peasantry. The experiment with democratization through mass education has failed, and the message of civilization, in achieving its widest audience, has moved toward entropy. The equal and opposite movement to balance the distortion of culture has stimulated the emergence of a new elite, not an elite in power and in control of postindustrial civilization, but an elite which can formulate an integral vision of culture and maintain the high standards of that culture without compromise to the forces of electronic vulgarization.

Since exoteric and esoteric are mirror-images of one another, the electronic masses attuned to television and the mystae attuned to the ancient esoteric mysteries are intimately related to one another. One group observes the electronic flow of information through all the television satellites around the world; the other group perceives the flow of information in the *akash*, the etheric structure of space-time itself.[2] For the mystae, the earth is a living being, and in the living electric ocean which flows around the earth in the noosphere there is a planetary consciousness directly available to the meditating initiate. For the adept of the world of consciousness, the mind is like an FM radio: as you turn the dial through meditation, different kinds of information and music come flooding in. But for the traditional man of letters, both the electronic peasant spaced out on rock music and the etheric initiate caught up in the music of the spheres are equally symptoms of the end of civilization.

The exoteric flow of information through television collectivizes and creates the mass, but the esoteric flow of information in the noosphere is anarchic. The mystical experience is absolutely universal and unique; it cannot be institutionalized, and every church or consciousness-raising hype which has tried to distribute it to a mass audience has succeeded only in caricaturing the experience it celebrates. Institutions can create conditions in which a transformation *may* possibly occur, but they cannot *cause* a transformation of consciousness. A university can provide you with a library, but what makes the book you are *not* looking for fall off the shelf into your hands to give you the material you need is not understood by any university. When a scientist receives a dream that gives him a breakthrough in his research, he has stepped to the side of his ego into those marginal areas of consciousness described by William James. In other words, he has moved out of the center to be everywhere at once in a peripheral consciousness. Since this movement away from analysis, separation, and control by the ego to peripheral scanning, pattern recognition, and intuitive awareness cannot be taught by the schools, the new elite of the new culture cannot be identified with the centers of postindustrial learning such as Harvard and MIT.

When the center cannot hold, mere anarchy is loosed upon the world; and so when there is a shift away from the ego in an individual or the collective ego, the political elite, there comes about a release of heat from the breakup of the old structures. We know this release of heat as terrorism.

This terrorism is a release of heat in a phase change, a transition from one culture to another. In civilization the center controlled the periphery; in planetary culture, in the words of the old Hermetic axiom, "the center is everywhere and the circumference nowhere," and hence there is no need for the periphery to strike back at the center through terrorism. As we look at terrorism now, it seems like the end of the world, for nothing is as fragile as a huge and powerful city like New York. With the projected ability of terrorists to make atom bombs, it seems as if we are beginning to see the end of the world. But perhaps a sense of history can help us see that we are entering a period, not of destruction, but destructuring.

In 1500 Hieronymus Bosch, a member of the mystical Brethren of the Free Spirit, painted the triptych of "The Last Judgment." Things were seen in the air dropping fire onto the burning cities; the sky was cracking open and Jesus was returning to judge the fallen world. In 1500 many people were afraid of that magical number and felt that they were going to see the end of the world, just as now many people are afraid that civilization will not live to see the year 2000. Well, the world did not end in 1500, but from another point of view, it did. For 1500 spelled the end of the high Middle Ages, the beginning of the age of exploration, the end of Christendom, and the rise of the modern world system in the new world economy. 1500 was the beginning of the shift from a centripetal, sacred world view to a centrifugal, secular world view; it was the beginning of the shift from Christian to commercial civilization. It was indeed the end of a world.

When you are living in a period of destructuring, the unconscious projects mythologies of destruction, for the unconscious can see time in hundreds and thousands of years. Since the artist or the prophet is more attuned to the unconscious, he can see and understand these vast stretches of time through myth. On the turning of the spiral, a form which brings 1500 and 2000 close together, Bosch could see the end of his world system and the end of our world system together as two turns of the spiral, two switchbacks on the long road of history only a short space apart.

We, like Bosch before us, cannot tell whether we are living in a period of literal destruction or of destructuring, perhaps because both processes are going on at once. If I were forced to make a guess, I would say that the next quarter century will see the destructuring of civilization, but not its apocalyptic destruction. I believe that many of us will still be around in the year 2000.

But the way in which we will be around, I believe, will be profoundly altered, and the way in which we can catch a glimpse of this alteration is through myth. What is happening in this world-order revolution in the shift from civilization to planetization is the return to the seasonal round, a return to connectedness with the biosphere, a shift from masculine, linear, binary modes of thought to feminine, cyclical, and analogical modes of being. In the scientific return to nature through New Alchemy, we return to our beginning in a new way; in the ancient myth the serpent bites its tail and releases the poison which cures it. Living in a period of chaos and disintegration, we experience the return of the most primitive beginning and watch it bite the end and release the unexpected agency of transformation. From the destructuring of civilization comes the unimaginable creation of planetization.

If in industrial society our identity was based upon our homes, our cars, our appliances, then in the new planetary culture our identity will be based upon a new arrangement of time and space in our very being. You are what you own in industrial society; in planetary culture, your being is what you are.

In postindustrial society the individual nuclear family was the archetypal unit. Enshrined in its split-level tract house, and empowered by all its new machines and appliances, it had no need for the community of the rural village or the old neighborhood in the city. But to make room for all those cars and appliances, the family had to be pared down to its essential minimum. If you are going to design a house with a garage for two cars, you do not have room for grandparents or aged aunts. You do not need people, for in postindustrial society you replace labor-intensive communities with energy-intensive technologies, and nothing is more energy-intensive than the suburban nuclear-family home. But from the weed-killer on the front lawn, to the plastics in the Tupperware in the automatically defrosting, ice-cube-making refrigerator, to the self-cleaning oven, the washer and dryer, the permanent-press polyester clothes, the no-iron sheets, the electric blanket, and the electric toothbrush, the suburban home is a fantasy way of life made out of oil. Like a growth hormone injected into a chicken to give it rapid, if carcinogenic growth, oil has been injected into the nuclear-family home, and a whole new way of life has sprung up in the generation from 1945 to 1974.

But it has not been only our homes; whole cities have been taken apart and put back together again to make room for the automobile and its attached house. Robert Moses rebuilt New York City to create suburban Nassau County, and General Motors helped to talk Los Angeles into dismantling its Pacific Electric train system so that people could drive to work on newer freeways. In every case, community was destroyed to make room for consumption.

And now all of that will be reversed, for "reversal is the movement of Tao." It takes no Amos or Jeremiah to pronounce a "woe to them that are at ease in Zion." People can read their fate in the morning papers. The postindustrial world we took for granted from 1945 to 1974 is over; the next thirty years will see a countermovement away from consumption to community.

People are going to have to come together in new communities of caring and sharing; they are going to have to give up many of their energy-intensive ways to return to labor. What will be necessary in the movement away from suburban society will be a turn on the spiral in a rediscovery of the preindustrial village.

The preindustrial village had a dynamic flexibility. Children and old people could work with the middle-aged in a responsible way; they were not collectivized in schools and nursing homes. Women were an enormously important part of the economy of a preindustrial village. A woman could nurse her baby and tend her loom, or work in a round of seasonal jobs which came up at different times of the year.[3] She could do her weaving, and then give it to the jobber who would come to her cottage to take her work to the marketplace. In the shift to economies of scale and the factory system, the jobber was turned into a shop foreman, the mother was turned into a unit in a production line, and the child was collectivized, first in factories and then in schools. The whole generalized adaptability of the woman was forced into specialization within the tiny ecological niche of the factory job. We know that to be generalized and to have multiple adaptability is a mark of evolutionary flexibility, and so industrialization can be seen as a specialized adaptation to a tiny ecological niche—in other words, a dead end.

What is true of women in preindustrial culture is equally true of old people. The rural craftsman could flourish in his trade until the day he died. We see something of this consciousness still lingering in the arts and the humanities:

think of Picasso, Frank Lloyd Wright, or A. N. Whitehead. Whitehead wrote all his greatest works in philosophy after his retirement from the University of London, when he came to a second career at Harvard. When aging is considered part of life, it becomes full of life; when old age is considered a living death, people die in the first year of their retirement. The fact that men die of heart disease and women of cancer of the uterus and breast is no mere accident but a profound indication that industrial society is destroying us in our most vital and life-affirming places.

A deep and affirming consciousness of death indicates a deep and affirming consciousness of life. In the shift from community to consumption, we became what we owned, and so alone with all our purchases, we became frightened and death became a hysterical obsession. Disconnected from nature and the human community, the isolated ego became terrified of its aloneness and sought a denial of death in massive collectivization in monstrous institutions. In gigantic and impersonal hospitals, the isolated ego looked to technology to deliver it from pain and death; and in the usual twist of opposites in life, the ego's very fear of pain and death put it in the hands of techniques of impersonal medical engineering, for which it paid dearly out of its stores of money. At hundreds of dollars a day, it was wired, plugged in, and plumbed with tubes, and bit by bit subjected to medical dismemberment. It says much about our society if we stop to think that probably each of us has had the experience of visiting a friend who was dying of cancer in a hospital.

The pathological distortions of our way of life are expressed in our way of dying. Because we know only the ego, we have lost the contemplative way of watching our breath, our joy, our pain, our life, our death. If we could let go of our ego and its possessions, and its possession of us, then we could be free to die in a contemplative leave-taking with friends and family around us.

Because postindustrial culture said, "You are what you own," it created an anxiety about possessions and encouraged people to replace their cars and homes regularly, lest they grow old. The aging of possessions began to be as threatening as age itself, but if a culture devotes itself to youth and newness, then the personal anxiety about being thrown away and becoming useless in that culture will increase as individuals keep changing cars, homes, and spouses, only to find themselves advancing into old age despite each new purchase on life. Southern California is the pre-eminent example of this culture of compulsive youth, a culture where the aged go to desperate attempts to look like Hollywood stars and spend small fortunes on cosmetic surgery; and so Southern California proves that where the whole way of life is devoted to consumption, it is people who become consumed.

Any way we care to look at postindustrial culture, from its supporting energy grid, its mores, or its informational systems, we can see that it has reached its limit. There is too much momentum in the mass and speed of California's rush to the end of the age, so it will probably continue on its course until the whole system blacks out; but in Vermont, or Prince Edward Island, or New Zealand, or Denmark there are already signs of the beginning of a shift from postindustrial to metaindustrial culture.

The shift will involve a movement away from fossil-fuel agribusiness to organic agriculture. Vermont now eats the produce of California; in the nineteenth century Vermont produced its own food. In the next quarter century Vermont will need to return to the production of its own food, for the costs of growing, freezing, cellophane-wrapping, and shipping the food from California to Vermont will become horrendous. This shift will not be an isolated one but a complete cultural shift from capital-intensive economies of scale which are net-energy inflationary to labor-intensive economies of regional modes of decentralized production. If resources are rare, and if every metal is a precious metal, then goods will have to become very good indeed. The world of built-in obsolescence and of heating up the economy through advertising will have to give way to an economy in which a power saw is built in a craft-guild workshop to last a hundred years. To produce such an instrument, we will need not an army of industrial proletarians in Detroit but a workshop of contemplatives crafting an instrument with Zen mindfulness. We will need to go back to the example of the Shakers to build every piece of furniture "as though you had a thousand years to live, and as if you were to die tomorrow."[4]

Since goods will be few, long-lasting, and costly, they will be beyond the reach of the isolated nuclear family. The community, and not the nuclear family, will have to become the basic unit of consumption. But in a community of "Right Livelihood" and appropriate technology, there will be more than enough to ensure a good life for the members of the community. The electric knife and toothbrush may be missing, but the tools needed for the growth of a rich culture will be at hand.

The energy grid for metaindustrial culture will not be the center-periphery system of fossil fuels but the anarchic flow of wind and sun, a flow in which "the center is everywhere and the circumference nowhere." The culture of fossil fuels literally feeds off the past, off the world of the dinosaurs, but the culture of solar energy feeds off light, and so the shift from the subterranean world of coal mine and oil well to the open horizons of wind and sun is really a shift in archetypes which will have profound repercussions in the collective unconscious. The political systems which are necessary to control the flow of water in Mesopotamia or the flow of oil in the modern world will no longer be necessary. With solar energy there will be enough power to create a good life, to support a community living in harmony with nature, but there will not be the concentrations of *power* to drive the old factory system. Solar energy will not give you the power to run Detroit or Las Vegas, or to put Coca-Cola in aluminum cans, or to jumbo-jet Ritz crackers to Caracas, and the fact that we are running out of energy for that ridiculous industrial culture is a blessing in disguise. The futurologists refuse to imagine anything but greater and greater expansions of the world industrial system, and so they dream of expensive solar collectors in space or huge solar farms in New Mexico or of a Promethean seizure of the power of the sun in thermonuclear fusion, but they are like junkies dreaming of the perfect fix: the very fantasy is likely to lead to the overdose which will kill them.

There is a value, however, to the futurology of Herman Kahn, for his visions enable us to see that futurology is merely the ideological camouflage of the Managers of the corporate industrial world. Fearful of a future that may not have a large enough place for them in it, they have cleverly, like Hollywood movie producers, bought up all the rights on the public images of the future by creating the Disneyland University of Futurology. There is no such science as futurology; to speak of the future is simply to discuss the implications of the present when everyone else is looking at the present but seeing the past.

To look at the present and describe what I see as going on is not an exercise in prophecy but simply looking, feeling, thinking, and meditating. The four activities come together in the unity of intuition. Out of that intuition, I would disagree with Herman Kahn's multifold trend, to say that there

are four archetypal forces at work today in the transformation of contemporary culture:

1. The planetization of nations
2. The decentralization of cities
3. The miniaturization of technology
4. The interiorization of consciousness

Teilhard de Chardin first observed the planetization of
nations in the 1940s, in his essay on the atom bomb. He
noted that the more the nations built armaments to separate
themselves and maintain their sovereign independence, the
more the very armaments forced them to come together in a
new international system. And so the planetization of nations is the emergence of a new world order. The opposite of
planetization is simply thermonuclear war. If we don't
achieve planetization, we cannot go back to an earlier era.
We have already entered into the rite of initiation; we cannot return to normalcy, for with the energies already
released, we would grow worse, not better. Once the demons are loosed, they cannot be put back; they have to be
transformed into deities.

The second force is the decentralization of cities. The
modern flow of information through satellites and electronic
media means the end to the kind of cities we have known in
the period from Uruk to New York. The polarity between
center and periphery is restructured in a new form of culture in which we can return to nature without going back to
"the idiocy of rural life." Like the biosphere, or the oceans,
or a superconductor, culture has now become a complex cir-
culating electrical fluid, a liquid crystal. In what Whitehead
called the "prehensive unification of space," every point is
involved with every other point, and a tiny Findhorn or
Auroville can be as important for cultural evolution as a
giant London or New York. The Sanskrit word for space is

akash, so we should see the prehensive unification of space as simply one modulation of consciousness, and the akash—or the akashic record, as Rudolf Steiner calls it—as simply a complex liquid crystal or superconductor in which information is stored and available to all who can meditate and attune themselves to it. Once again, the akash is a space in which "the center is everywhere and the circumference nowhere." If the center is everywhere, then there is no single elite at the center.

The opposite force to decentralization is, of course, urbanization, and if we do not decentralize, then all our cities will become like Calcutta, and the center-periphery dialectic of civilization will reach its extreme polarization in dictatorship and terrorism. If civilization is not transformed, it will explode.

The third societal force is the miniaturization of technology. I believe that this overlooked shift in the scale of man to machine has profound implications for cultural evolution. If the machines are small and people can once again hear the trees, then the sensibility goes through a profound revolution and the relationship between culture and nature changes dramatically. The miniaturization of technology enables us to reduce the scale of the impact of industrialization on the biosphere. In a shift from hardware to information, from capital-intensive economies of scale to communal forms of regional production, from consumer values to contemplative values, the industrial maladjustment to nature is corrected and the neurotic compulsions of modern society are alleviated.

The opposite of the miniaturization of technology is the exponential growth of giantism, bureaucracy, and the technologizing of human beings in a totally mechanized culture in which all things natural are looked upon as atavisms left over from an uncompleted evolution. As gigantic and com-

plex machines become the dominant features of our landscape, the rule of experts becomes unavoidable, and therefore many technocrats, such as Zbigniew Brzezinski and
Simon Ramo, argue for a world in which the citizen is separated from the political process by the introduction of advanced management systems which he cannot possibly hope
to understand. In the cybernetic state of high technology,
the citizen becomes the subject, and the bread and circuses
of a guaranteed annual income and color television keeps
him happy in his cubicle in the megalopolis.

> According to Simon Ramo, founder of TRW, a suc-
> cessful high-technology firm, technology is an in-
> strument for predicting the future and solving so-
> cial problems. Because man "must now plan on
> sharing the earth with machines," he must "alter
> the rules of society, so that we and they can be
> compatible."[5]

Because most technocrats are linear thinkers, they do not
understand the dialectic of opposites; they cannot see that
electronics and high technology are reversing the processes
of urbanization and industrialization. In the scientific return
to nature through New Alchemy, the compatibility of man
and machine is not the postindustrial landscape of MIT or
Apollo 17 but the electronics and animism of a new-age
community like Findhorn. Hand-held calculators and desk-
top computers use a fraction of the energy of old technologies, and so advanced science is now possible even in wilderness situations. A scientist at work in a laboratory in
which everything is controlled inevitably projects those systems of control on the state, but a scientist at work in nature
who is sensitive to the life "of all sentient beings" projects
that sensitivity into his political relations. The science of a
Jane van Lawick-Goodall or a John Todd does not become

the political science of a Simon Ramo or a Zbigniew Brze-zinski.

The fourth societal force is the interiorization of consciousness. In the emergence of the modern world in the sixteenth century, there was a shift from the concentric, centripetal orientation of medieval Christendom to the centrifugal expansions in the age of humanism, exploration, and science. This orientation still continues in the exploration of space. The externalization of consciousness leads the individual to look for all values outside: the next frontier contains the solution to all the disappointments of the last frontier. You move to the New World, cut down its forests, pollute its great lakes, and then look to Australia, Brazil, or LaGrange Place V in space. Now, however, we can sense the beginning of the end of the masculine mode of externalization. Several of the astronauts have had mystical conversion experiences from their journeys into space, and the men trained by NASA to be appendages to their high-technology systems have returned to earth with a profound sense of the mystical dimensions of human evolution. It is likely that for whatever motivation that may impell human beings into space, from a lust for power or a desire simply for corporate profits from aerospace contracts, the cultural implication of the exploration of space will be the opposite of that intended. In a good Yeatsian fashion, the maximum expansion of the frontier in external space will open up the opposite dimension of internal space. St. Paul thought he knew his reasons for traveling to Damascus, but he was knocked off his horse by a power beyond his control. In a similar fashion, on Apollo 9, the failure of a camera gave astronaut Russell Schweickart a moment to float freely in space and contemplate the earth. That moment, like a religious conversion experience, changed his life. He was free to look down at the earth and know it from the inside out.[6]

The interiorization of consciousness is a change in values in which we begin to look for the source of the good life within rather than without. Culturally, this change in orientation would express itself as a return to the centripetal and concentric qualities of medieval society. In the Middle Ages, the larger symbolic envelopment of society was Christendom, but the way in which Christendom was realized was not in the nation-state, but in the feudal manor or the village. In the new culture, the planet will be the larger symbolic envelopment, not the nation-state, but the way in which the planet will be experienced will be through the metaindustrial village. As we move up to a larger scale in one frame of reference, there is a need to move down to a closer and more intimate level on another. This scale need not be exclusively focused on villages, for in planetary culture it may mean more emotionally to be Quebecois than Canadian, Welsh rather than British, or a New Yorker rather than an American. But whether the individual is in a city or a village, I imagine that his values will be contemplative and not consumptive, ecological and not industrial.

If we do not achieve the interiorization of consciousness in our culture, then the result will be the continuing externalization of our sickness in pollution and catastrophic disruption of the biosphere from industrial and nuclear wastes. The law of opposites will play itself out, and the heating up of the atmosphere from global industrial development will alter the biosphere and disrupt the whole basis of industrial civilization.

Each of the four societal forces has its equal and opposite force. If we don't achieve the planetization of nations, we will have thermonuclear war. If we don't achieve the decentralization of cities, then London, Paris, and New York will go the way of Calcutta. (You have only to read Doris Lessing's novel *Memoirs of a Survivor* to get a sense of what the future of the megalopolis is likely to be.) And if we don't achieve the miniaturization of technology, we will experience the technologizing of human beings, and an authoritarian government with a scientific elite will rule over the electronic peasantry through the propaganda of such television programs as *The Six Million Dollar Man*. Then we will not turn on the spiral close to the spirit of the Middle Ages, but back further, close to the spirit of the dying Roman Empire.

The imperial vision of the future is precisely what you have in the work of Herman Kahn. The latifundia of the decadent Empire have been replaced by multinational corporations, but the outlines of a pathological giantism are similar. With a projected 15 billion people on the planet, each earning an alleged $20,000 a year, Kahn sees the world as all business executives do: unending markets, unending profits, unending industrialization. By contrast, I believe that the population of the earth will actually *decline* over the next century. Meteorologists have indicated that we are entering a new period of cold weather, and that the last cycle has been an unusually warm spell. This period of planetary good weather has been associated with the population increases that preceded the Industrial Revolution. If we are entering a new cold period, and this climatic change is occurring right at the time of a fuel crisis, then the new demands of heating, coming at a time of increased demands for fossil-fuel fertilizers, insecticides, and oil for tractors, trucks, and combines, will create a global crisis for agribusiness, the balance of trade payments, and currency values. Since we have only twenty-odd days' worth of food stored on the planet, it would only take a few cold winters coupled with a few summer droughts to devastate the industrial civilization of planet earth. In America we would then discover to our grief just what it means to live in an oil-based postindustrial society in which 98 per cent of the population are not involved in food production.

We can see how unnatural postindustrial civilization is if we look back at a few historical figures. In 1800 more than 90 per cent of the American population lived in rural areas; even as late as 1880, two thirds of the people lived in the country. But by 1950 two thirds of the population lived in cities.[7] If you don't believe in the possibilities of change, just stop to consider that dramatic and archetypal move from the country to the city. Well, if a social movement can go in one direction, it can also go in the other. I believe that by the year 2000 we are going to have to have one half of our population living in rural areas. Assuming that we do not experience a catastrophic return to the Dark Ages, I see the return to the country as the creation of a new metaindustrial culture and not a return to preindustrial agrarian society.

But perhaps I had better define my terms. Using only a single parameter, namely, the distribution of population in sections of the economy, we can get a good idea of the meaning of the terms preindustrial, postindustrial, and metaindustrial.

PERCENTAGE OF POPULATION INVOLVED IN OCCUPATIONS

Preindustrial		*Industrial* (*U.S.A. in 1900*)	
Agriculture	80%	Agriculture	38%
Industry	10%	Industry	38%
Services	10%	Services	24%

Postindustrial (U.S.A. in 1972)		Metaindustrial (U.S.A. in 2000)	
Agriculture	4%	Agriculture	40%
Industry	32%	Industry	20%
Services	64%	Services	40%

From 1900 to 1972 America experienced a shift in population from agriculture and industrial production to services, and this shift, supported by massive injections of oil, is what postindustrial civilization is all about. In America the most highly populated profession is teaching, and so it is fair to say that we live in a world of information, not of farms or factories. To appreciate the unusual nature of our civilization, we should consider the fact that in Maoist China, 96 per cent of the population is involved in food production. The Chinese have factories and high-technology laboratories, but they do not have freeways, McDonald's stands, and shopping centers.

Now what I am saying is that there are four levels not three, and I am departing from the futurology of Herman Kahn by seeing the fourth cultural level as metaindustrial rather than superindustrial. *Meta-* is a prefix derived from Greek used to mean "beyond," and what I am envisioning from experiments like New Alchemy in Cape Cod and the Farallones Institute in California is a society beyond Los Angeles and Detroit. Postindustrial society, which the good Dr. Kahn sees as going on forever, is based on oil and capital-intensive economies of scale, but we are now beginning to experience both shortages of oil and capital, and so I am projecting not a linear extrapolation but a more complex dialectic, a dialectic in keeping with historical knowledge and the wisdom of the ancient Taoist who noted that "reversal is the movement of Tao."

I am assuming that by the year 2000 the electronic decentralization of information and the miniaturization of technology will enable people to move from New York, Detroit, and Los Angeles to live in rural areas. I am assuming that the production of good small tools will enable communities to produce goods and services in small workshops rather than large factories. I am assuming that the existence of electronics, as expressed in informational flow and miniaturized technology, will enable society to appreciate the prophetic visions of Piotr Kropotkin rather than Karl Marx. I am also assuming that, as human beings begin to move out of the concrete world of New York to live with trees, the consciousness of the individual will undergo a profound transformation in a scientific return to animism.

If you want to be more poetic than demographic, then you can identify metaindustrial culture as one in which the trees are counted in a census of the members of the community. Trees breathe what we exhale and exhale what we breathe; they are the very blood cells of the biosphere which nourish all parts of the planet. When the Sumerian king Gilgamesh killed the great spirit of the forest, Humbaba, he became possessed with the fear of death and tried to lock out nature with the great wall of Uruk. Gilgamesh is the great and pathetic hero of civilization, but now at the end of civilization we are beginning to understand the failures of heroes, cities, and great military walls. The spirit of the forest haunts us, and will continue to do so until we give it a new life in the heart of a new human culture.

Metaindustrial culture is not the culture of the industrial lumberjack with his screaming power saw but the culture of the poet, the ecologist, the "primitive" animist who asks the tree's permission before he uses it. It is a culture in which death and life are seen together, and in which humans return to the trees what they take for their own needs. Everything in nature gives in its death; stars die and whole solar systems begin to evolve from the impregnation of the exploded stellar matter. Trees die, and from their wood human beings build homes and furniture, statues and Stradivariuses. If humans died in a healthy culture, they would not lock out the earth in metal coffins and carve their names on stone monuments, but would instead place the naked body in the earth and plant a tree above the silent heart.

The movement from the city to the country is not simply a movement in physical space, but a transformation of the individual's being in space. We may not be able to experience metaindustrial culture without ecological catastrophe, famine, economic collapse, and thermonuclear war, but it is the work of writers to suggest visions of a way of life before the disaster is upon us. Whether Wordsworth or D. H. Lawrence, A.E. or Prince Kropotkin, the writer has his daimon and has no choice in going against the current of his entire civilization. When the writer is a historian, the work becomes a bit more difficult, for he can look back to the past and see that society did not listen to Wordsworth, Lawrence, A.E., or Kropotkin, that the probabilities of catastrophe increase with each year; but for all his historical knowledge, he too has no choice: he must work in the assumption that there is a chance for a dramatic conversion experience, a chance for a new planetary life in the face of a new planetary death.

And so I imagine a transformation from the present postindustrial civilization to a new planetary, metaindustrial culture. I imagine a movement in America in which 40 per cent of the population become involved with food production. If in the near future we begin to experience a shortage of food, then the sacredness of food will have to be rediscovered, and that resacralization will have to be part of an individual's education. As in Mao's China, or in the spiritual community of Findhorn in Scotland, the students and teachers will have to work in the fields as well as in the libraries.

Not only will colleges have to become like the community of Findhorn, but factories will also. In a shift from the old factory system, which alienates women from the productive process and workers from management, factories will need to become communities with workers on the board of directors of the local and autonomous small plant. With an emphasis on contemplative and communal values, the goods would be crafted to be good and long-lasting, after the traditions of the Shakers.

Evolution occurs in small populations or *demes* in which a mutation has taken place. The metaindustrial village is just such a deme; it is a place in which the four cultural forces are completely expressed. The metaindustrial village is a turn on the spiral back toward the preindustrial village, *but it is not* the preindustrial village; for with electronics, complex informational flow on a global level, and higher states of consciousness from a contemplative education, it is not a return to "the idiocy of rural life." If there is not a complex informational flow which relates the village to the planet, then you do not have a metaindustrial village but simply a regressive hippie commune. A community without a planetary informational flow in the form of telephones, satellite and cable television, and computer terminals is like a pond without a feeding stream: the ecosystem becomes stagnant. There is no such thing as a self-sufficient and closed ecosystem; everything in nature flows through everything else. The openness to time and space in the village is important, for people fled the country to have the freedom of the city. If people move into communes to escape the problems of the city but have no larger vision than that of escape, they constellate a collective neurosis in which the community has no cultural content other than their neurotic relationships to one another.

What will enable the metaindustrial village to be more than a stagnant pond is the interiorization of consciousness, through new forms of contemplative education, and the miniaturization of technology. With desk-top computers and microfiche libraries, advanced science will be possible in the most rural, even wilderness circumstances. The technology that enables research to go on in a tiny space station also enables research to go on in a remote wilderness. In the usual enantiodromia of historical movements, the developments of the factory system and complex projects such as Apollo stimulate their opposite in the shift away from the factory system in the culture as a whole.

Now I am not arguing that the appearance of the metaindustrial village will spell the death of all large projects. In ecological terms, I am projecting a movement from a *succession-forest* kind of economy to a *climax-forest* economy in the global, centripetal reconsolidation of planetary culture. I am assuming that there will be a continued sublimation of the military-industrial complex into co-operative Soviet and American projects in space. I am fully aware that the dynamic of opposites can mean that allegedly peaceful space colonies can become a means to prolong the life of the corporate factory system, and that the space colonies could become, as Dennis Meadows has suggested, like nuclear submarines in the sky. If we do not transform industrial society, then the colonies simply become metastatic carcinomas, a necklace of tumors encircling the cancer-stricken earth. But the kind of dynamic of opposites I am hoping for is one in which a space technology makes the metaindustrial village possible, and the village, as a new form of college, transforms the consciousness of the scientists involved with governments and space exploration. Since everything is involved with everything, no expert can predict how new developments will work out. Engineers and chemists created television and LSD, and a generation of hippies appeared on the scene. The hippies did not convert America to a simpler life style, but they did influence the advertising executives of Madison Avenue, who began to smoke marijuana and produce rock-inspired commercials that helped to shoot speed into the consumer culture of America. In the sixties there were only a handful of short-lived communes, but the hippie capitalism of *Rolling Stone* magazine and the giant record companies had a much greater impact on the establishment. If hippies can help stimulate the corporate-capitalistic system, then, obviously, space colonies can end up doing anything from saving the military-industrial system from bankruptcy to hijacking the earth and holding the U.S.A. and the Soviet Union as hostages to force the earth into adopting a world government under the aegis of the United Nations.

Nevertheless, an appreciation for the concept of enantiodromia enables you to make a few educated guesses about the future. Giant factories created tiny instruments like hand-held calculators and desk-top computers. A computer that once filled an enormous room that had to be air-conditioned and climatically controlled can now be run on batteries. If technology can be scaled down, then nature can be scaled up, and once we begin to live with trees, the animism of the American Indians and my ancestral Druids is going to return in a wholly new context.

The first experience I had of the miniaturization of technology and the decentralization of cities came while I was teaching at MIT. While young professors like myself had to drive through the rush-hour traffic to get to work, the Institute Professors in computer science could stay out at their farms in Lincoln, Massachusetts, for they had been given computer terminals in their studies as a reward for their contributions to the Institute. In an inverse snobbery, the more advanced you were, the more you could avoid the center to be a hick at the periphery. In the words of the economist Kenneth Boulding, it was a situation in which the rich walked and the poor had to drive. Since Los Angeles has grown up because of the automobile and the availability of cheap oil, it takes no prophet to predict that the shortages of fuel and capital mean that the Los Angelization of the planet is, happily, not a likely prospect for the future.

The decentralization of cities and the miniaturization of technology will alter the center-periphery dialectic of traditional civilization and make a whole new cultural level possible. What will take place in the metaindustrial village will be that the four classical economies of human history, hunting and gathering, agriculture, industry, and cybernetics, will all be recapitulated within a single deme. We will look back to where we have been in history, gather up all the old economies, and then turn on the spiral in a new direction.

The hunting and gathering economy could focus on the gathering of wood, wind, and sun. In a way, the work of the New Alchemy Institute is to create a food and energy base for a small tribal band of people living in isolated circumstances. As sociologist Elise Boulding has remarked, "I sometimes wonder if our motto today does not need to be: 'Forward to the Paleolithic!' The folk of the Neolithic, with their cozy farm communities, working like dogs and breeding like rabbits, have little that is useful to say to us."[8] New Alchemy is not a civilized strategy; it is not going to feed the huddled masses of New York and Calcutta; it either will be co-opted and absorbed by conglomerate NASA as the ecology of a space colony or will enable small groups to live in dispersed settlements—or both.

The agricultural economy of the metaindustrial village

would focus on organic gardening and the replacing of fossil-fuel agribusiness with natural cycles in the food chain. Since the shift from gardening to field tillage with the plow originally displaced women from food production, the return to ecologically sophisticated gardening enables women to return to take up significant roles in the economy of the village, and thus to overcome the sexual alienation characteristic of industrial society.

The third economy of the community would be industrial, and this is where I part company with many critics of contemporary culture. The metaindustrial village is not anti-industrial and Luddite; there will be industry and technology, but they will be brought down to scale as workshops in converted barns. A village could produce artistically beautiful glass bottles which could be kept as art objects or reused as containers in place of plastics. Or the village could produce bicycles, clothing, rotary tillers, or other well-crafted and durable instruments. In a return to the mystery of the craft guild, particular communities could focus on the revival of particular crafts and industries. Whatever the industry chosen, the scale of the operation would be small, in harmony with the ecosystem of the region, and devoted more to a local market than an international one.

The fourth economy of the community would be postindustrial, or cybernetic. The characteristic feature of a postindustrial economy is the emphasis on research and development and education. Since the entire village would be a contemplative educational community, after the manner of Lindisfarne and Findhorn, the adventure of consciousness would be more basic to the way of life than patterns of consumption. Everyone living in the community would be involved in an experiential approach to education, from contemplative birth, after the thought of Dr. Frederick LeBoyer, to contemplative death, after the thought of Dr.

Elizabeth Kübler-Ross. And at the various stages of life in between, the entire community would function as a college, in which children and adults would work together in gardening, construction, ecological research, crafts, and classes in all fields of knowledge. These educational communities already exist in places like Auroville in India, Findhorn in Scotland, and Lindisfarne in New York, but none of these communities has yet achieved the miniaturization of the four classical economies of human history into a single deme.

The importance of such miniaturization is that this compression makes human evolution visible in a new way, and thus allows a new evolution of consciousness to take place. When you look back at something, you are already out of it and moving into a new environment. The four economies already exist together on the planet, and the planet from an evolutionary point of view is a single deme, but this planetary level of awareness is not available as a direct experience for many people. A few mystics such as David Spangler and a few scientists such as the astronaut Russell Schweickart have had an experience of planetary consciousness, but the majority of humanity is restricted to quite narrow perspectives. By making the small human community into a microcosm of the planet, the community itself becomes a *yantra*, an object of contemplation for insight into universal processes of evolution and transformation. What MIT was to postindustrial society, the metaindustrial village will become for the new culture.

The miniaturization of the four economies is an exoteric social process that can be understood in a conventional fashion; but there is also an esoteric mystery at work here. Students of esoteric theology, whether they are students of Findhorn, Sri Aurobindo, Rudolf Steiner, or Alice Bailey will understand what I am going to say, but for others, the following will seem absurd. In their case, I would ask that they remember Albert Camus's remark, "The absurd is lucid reason stating its limits."

Everything in the universe from quarks to quasars is alive; consciousness is not an object simply located in the skull of *Homo sapiens* but is a universal field, occasions of which can be experienced, in a very limited way, by human beings. The chain of being is such that an organization at one level attracts consciousness at another. When musicians come together to play improvisationally, they can discover a peculiar spirit that manifests when they are playing in an inspired fashion. What happens cannot be explained away by the signs and signals of subtle body language; something else happens, and that something is the manifestation of a group consciousness. The members of the string quartet become a single mind; they do not lose their individuality, but they begin to see the individual mind as *figure* against the *ground* of the collective mind. When the four classical economies of evolution come together, something else happens, and that something else is the emergence of the collective consciousness of the human species. The planet itself evolves a central nervous system, which is humanity, and opens its eyes to become conscious of an entirely new level of its existence in the universe.

At Findhorn the evolutionary synthesis is not expressed as the integration of the four economies but of the four kingdoms, mineral, vegetal, animal, and human. When the kingdoms come together in a single, consciously harmonious unity, a symmetry is created, a form, a vessel, and this vessel becomes filled with being from a higher level. The phenomenon is like a great concert: when all the musicians come together, something else enters the concert hall. Call it angel or muse, Christ or the god Apollo, *genius loci* or folk-soul, but the important thing is to realize that integration at one level of the chain of being enables modes of being at higher levels to manifest themselves. In the evolutionary theology of Sri Aurobindo, the ensouling is called "the descent of the supramental."[9] In the traditional Christian theology of St. Paul, the ensouling is called "the mystical body of Christ." The evolving earth is "the grail," and as the planet is filled by the logos of the sun, a new level of consciousness is achieved. But since this phenomenon is invisible, for we are like dots in a photograph who cannot see the picture in which they take their place, I had better return to cultural phenomena which can be seen on a historical scale.

A transformation of consciousness is now beginning to express itself in the field of theoretical architecture. Since architecture is the collective unconscious made visible, the architect himself does not always understand the full cultural implications of his own work. What is beginning to happen in architecture that is of interest to cultural historians like myself is the shift from postindustrial constructions of the Bauhaus International style to a symbiotic architecture in which the form is not a celebration of *power over* new materials, as was the case with aluminum and glass, but a celebration of *co-operation with* ecosystems, as is the case with the New Alchemy Ark in Prince Edward Island designed by Solsearch.[10] In the still-theoretical "bioshelter" of Day Charoudhi and Sean Wellesley-Miller, an attempt is being made to create a house that is "a domestication of an ecosystem."[11] The relationship between culture and nature is changed, for the architect does not simply stick a house in the ground, but, after the fashion of the ancient science of geomancy or *feng-shui*,[12] he spends a full year studying the land, the seasonal flow of its subtle energies, its flora and fauna, and then slowly he grows a house the way he would grow a garden.

In northern climates the thrust of architecture has been to

lock out nature with an iron wall, but in the new symbiotic architecture there is a shift from the iron wall to a light-permeable membrane. The structure is surrounded with a membrane and a cloud gel within the membrane that lets in light and stores heat. Across this membrane, as across the membrane of a living cell, information can pass, but it is information that respects the integrity of the living cell or the living house. In *The Lives of a Cell*, Dr. Lewis Thomas taught us to see the entire earth as a single living cell, and now the ramifications of this biological consciousness are being expressed in architecture.

Since science, literature, and architecture are all related to "the climate of thought" of an age, it is possible to see the archetypal quality of this change in forms. Ecology and symbiotic architecture both express a turning away from masculine, industrial, and dominating forms of thought to feminine, metaindustrial, and naturally co-operative modes of being. The house surrounded with a light-permeable membrane is the architecture of the womb, and like the womb, and unlike our modern houses which consume energy, the symbiotic house produces the food and energy needed by its inhabitants.

The political implications of such a system are, of course, enormous, and, once again, they express a shift from masculine forms of military dominance, the structure of the hydraulic civilizations of the urban revolution, to neolithic, feminine villages dedicated to the Great Goddess, Gaia.[13] Once again, we must remember that history is a spiral and not a circle. We are not going back to the neolithic village of Çatal Hüyük; we are not going back to the prehistoric matriarchy, so there is no need for men to tremble in terror with visions of Amazons or the beehive; there is no need to rush out to join the marines or the Ku Klux Klan to assert the sunset effect of machismo. In returning in historically novel ways to the cosmic feminine principle, our culture is simply righting the imbalance of the last five thousand years. The metaindustrial village will not be a "Lesbian Nation" or a beehive but an open community with planetary informational flow in which more highly individuated men and women realize through their contemplative way of life a happier balance of the masculine and feminine, *anima* and *animus,* within the Self.

It is always unsettling and annoying for one culture to see a subculture within its own society; it is all well and good to travel to some exotic and exciting culture halfway round the world, but when an alien way of life sprouts up in your own back yard it feels as if crab grass is invading the family turf. Sometimes when people see another culture, they make a move, but since such moves are full of risks, it is always very few people who are willing to undertake such risks.

And yet risk-taking is what evolution is all about. Some people prefer to take risks with the survival of the human species by gambling on nuclear power; others prefer to take risks with their own way of life. By 1984 we should be at the fork in the road. Then everyone should be able to see clearly the choice we need to make. One road will lead toward nuclear power, strip mining, and authoritarian governments which can underwrite the contracts for the corporations and the pension funds of the labor unions, as well as protect industrial society from revolution and terrorism. The other road will lead toward a spiritual awakening on the level of the great universal religions that have guided the cultural evolution of humanity. This path will be expressed by a change of heart and mind, a new wedding of nature and culture, and a new kind of human community which can express the resacralization of earth. With solar collectors contrasted with smog, smokestacks with windmills, meditators with teenagers with radios blasting in their ears as they walk the crowded streets, I hope that Americans will look at the two roads and choose the wisdom of the poet Gary Snyder, "to live lightly on the earth." Whichever choice we make, we will get what we deserve.

The historian Eric Hobsbawm has noted that the poets understood industrial society more quickly than the experts on parliamentary commissions.[14] Perhaps we can believe that the poets are understanding the new metaindustrial culture before the experts like Herman Kahn even know what is truly happening. The poet Gary Snyder sees a coming return to the paleolithic seasonal round in which computer-programmers walk with the elk. The poet Richard Brautigan also sees a landscape of animals and electronics, in his poem "All Watched Over by Machines of Loving Grace."

We are turning on a spiral and looking back to the neolithic village and the paleolithic seasonal round to go forward in a new direction, into a new culture that is an *Aufheben* of all the terrestrial cultures we have ever known. Toward that new planetary culture we each make different contributions. Lindisfarne's contribution is the attempt to reinterpret contemporary culture and provide a context for all the separate activities going on around the world. The metaindustrial village does not yet exist. Findhorn is working on the spiritual group-consciousness and sacred gardening, but not the science. New Alchemy is working on the scientific aspects, but New Alchemy is not a community. Lindisfarne is working on the philosophy and educational aspects, but it does not have the spiritual power of Findhorn or the science and appropriate technology of New Alchemy. What is needed for the metaindustrial village is a community in which the achievements of Findhorn, New Alchemy, and Lindisfarne are brought together. Zen Center in San Francisco and the Sufi Community in New Lebanon, New

York, are already making steps in this direction. The Buddhists have a monastery, a farm, a grocery store, a bakery, and the Alaya Stitchery as a cottage industry. The Sufis have a farm and a studio for the assemblage of computers. So there are some signs in the cultural evolution of America that, while the cold-blooded dinosaurs are tearing up the landscape, there are some tiny mammals around with warm blood in their hearts.

THREE

THE
RETURN
OF THE
PAST

IF YOU ARE GOING to think about the problem of time within a civilized, literate culture, there are basically two different ways to look at it. One is through myth; the other is through history. History, by definition, is a civilized, literate record of events; it is a conscious self-image of a society projected by an elite. In a sense, history is the self-image of a culture, the ego of a culture. History is controlled through education and tradition, and is monitored, if not manipulated, by elitist institutions, whether these are temples, academies, or universities. History is the story told by the elite in power and is a way of articulating human time so that it reinforces the institutional power of the elite. One of the ways the British maintained Ireland as a colony was through the writing of history. The actual role of the Irish monks and the Irish centers of learning in maintaining knowledge in the Dark Ages was blanked out, and on that blank slate even brilliant men like David Hume wrote that there was no culture in Ireland until it was brought in by the conquering Normans in the twelfth century. So historical consciousness is closely related to power and the ego of a society. For these reasons, Voltaire said that "history is the lie commonly agreed upon," and Marx, continuing in that vein, said that "the ruling ideas are in every age the ideas of the ruling class."

The tyrannies of history, however, do not always come from conscious malevolence. Equally important are the unconscious assumptions of the historian. What is not seen by the historian often shapes the entire way he looks out at the sequence of human events. This blindness is not always a product of inferior eyesight but may come from superior eyesight; it is the expertise of the historian which enables him to squint into a microscope and blind himself to everything else around him. If a historian focuses on baptismal registers in a rural shire in the last quarter of the eighteenth century, he may or may not be able to see the demographic shifts of the Industrial Revolution. But more often than not, specialists agree to talk with other specialists about their specialties, and so professional historians, held in tenure by temples, academies, or universities, purchase their tunnel vision with peripheral blindness.

Myth is the mirror-opposite of history. Myth is not the story of the ego of a civilization but the story of the soul. If you apply the terminology of C. G. Jung, you can say that myth is the story of the higher Self and that history is the story of the ego. If the ego has a limited perspective on matters and always sees things through its own passions and desires, then it is not going to be concerned with the larger perspective of the evolution of humanity or the nature of divinity. Myth, by contrast, is the larger picture. To think big is to think mythically. If you are going to ask the primordial questions—Who are we? Where do we come from? Where are we going?—then you are going to fall into mythic patterns of thinking in formulating the answers. Even in constructing a scientific narrative and articulating the known facts, the narrative will fall into a mythic pattern and archetypal structures will surface out of the unconscious.

Because we live in a culture in which the elite are scientists, we have been colonized to think that scientific and mythopoeic forms of thought are incompatible. Myth, we are told, is irrational and a vestige of earlier stages of human existence, but now that science has finally achieved the creation of a new culture, we will begin to see religion and myth slowly fade out of the picture in a process of increasing secularization and increasing rationalization. This is the argument put forth by A. F. C. Wallace in his book *Religion: An Anthropological Study*. This kind of thinking in the social sciences is picked up by futurologists such as Herman Kahn and spread into policy studies and governmental task forces. Herman Kahn's "multifold trend" is simply the social-science vision of time; it is a *history* of the future, a story told by the managerial elite of a technological society. If history is the lie commonly agreed upon, then futurology is the illusion commonly agreed upon.

One of the illusions commonly agreed upon by the elite of our society is that the scientific method is rational, and that myth and science are totally unrelated modes of thought. But if you look into the role of the imagination in scientific discovery, and look into the kinds of people who do the discovering, then you find that many of the great scientists were mystics and visionaries. The litany of Kepler, Descartes, Pascal, Newton, Faraday, Einstein, Schrödinger, and Heisenberg is not a roll call of scientific materialists but of mystics and Pythagoreans. But you do not have to be a card-carrying mystic to think mythically; you only have to think big to find yourself thinking mythically. When the physicist John Wheeler talks about black holes, he begins projecting images of terror, of black pits in space gobbling up gravity-collapsing stars. Where someone else might see death and rebirth, or portals to other dimensions, Wheeler sees only a myth of death and destruction. However, when Arthur C.

Clarke considers black holes, he sees doorways to other universes; the monolith in orbit around Jupiter in the film *2001*, Clarke told me was a black hole, a rent in space-time which enabled the astronaut to move into another world. So whether we see a black hole as menacing and demonic, a cosmic *vagina dentata*, or as transformational and positive depends on our unconscious assumptions about the nature of life and death, continuity and discontinuity, time and space. And these notions of existence are not so much the *contents* of knowledge that come to us from history and science as the *structures* of consciousness that come to us from myth.

If you listen to Werner Heisenberg lecturing about Pythagoreanism in his own work on the quantum theory, you will hear him emphasize that the basic building blocks of nature are number and pattern, that the universe is not made out of matter but out of music. The historians of science I worked with in the university regarded Pythagoras as a magician, a shamanistic madman from the cults of the Near East; yet both Whitehead and Heisenberg regarded him as a genius of the highest order who laid the foundation upon which our entire Western civilization is based.

At the level of the equator, science, religion, and art may seem to be hemispheres apart, but as you move up from the equator into higher levels of generalization, the longitudinal lines converge at the pole, as Teilhard de Chardin has pointed out. At this imaginary north pole, you have the region of mythopoeic thought, so that when the artist sits down to talk with the physicist, each can understand the other. The economist may not be able to understand the physicist; the politician may not be able to understand the artist; but the speculative physicist and the artist are familiar with the world of the imagination, and so they can become familiar with one another. Technicians are locked into the perspectives of their expertise; they have been trained, not educated, and so they can only interpret the world through their training. With rigidity and arrogance, the expert projects his pet theory and tries to force everything down under a grid. The creative scientist, the one who takes up the old anomalies and envisions the new paradigm, is by contrast a more open and receptive mind. Many times in the history of science, this receptivity on the part of the discoverer has been marked by an openness to the unconscious through which the new model appears in a dream. Whether in the theory of evolution, the model of the benzene ring, or the model of the atom, dreams and the unconscious have had their part to play in the history of scientific discovery.

Now because we live in a culture of scientific materialism, we are all brought up to believe certain common assumptions about the nature of progress and the high level of our technological society. In celebrations of the idea of technological progress, myth has been kicked out the front door but has sneaked in through an open window in the back in the disguise of science fiction. In a society organized around the idea of technological progress, science fiction is a tolerable way in which forbidden ideas can be entertained. The old worlds of religious myths and fairy tales have an interest for Jungians and other antiquarians, but our children are more familiar with *Star Trek* than Grimm's fairy tales. And so the cultural historian of our time must take science fiction very seriously to see it as the mythology of our age.

If you look at the movie *2001: A Space Odyssey* as a myth, you can begin to recognize it as a variant of Gnostic myths of the Fall. We ourselves are the star creatures from other dimensions who intersect with the time-space of the hominids, and enter history to begin the long march back to cosmic consciousness. In Kriya Yoga the chela is taught to meditate on the white five-pointed star to go out through that "star gate" to cosmic consciousness; and so when in the film the astronaut makes the journey to Jupiter in a spinal-column-looking ship, comes to the star gate, and then goes out to another universe, he is basically making the soul's journey familiar to all Kriya yogis. On the other side of birth and death, he becomes a messianic star-child who returns to earth to save mankind at a time as critical as the first descent of the soul into the body of the early hominids. And so the descent of the soul into the body of *Homo sapiens* on earth is a signal of a whole new quantum leap in human evolution.

Since most people in our culture are not students of Kriya Yoga or scholars of Gnosticism, the film is taken as science fiction, but that is simply like smuggling a book through customs by putting another cover on it. Once the book is through customs, the unconscious takes off the silly wrapper and recognizes the thing for what it is. Neither Kubrick nor Clarke is an initiate, but both are cultural mediums, and the medium does not have to understand the material which takes hold of it. At the unconscious level, however, Kubrick is artistically aware of the archetypal material, for he has emphasized it in the numinosity of the images which take on religious overtones because of the musical score. As the astronauts unearth the monolith on the moon, Bach's B Minor Mass is played in barely recognizable form through an electronic mixer and synthesizer. The procession of the astronauts to the cosmic tablet is a ritual in a mystery. I have talked to Clarke about the film, and he will not admit to the mystical dimensions of his own novel, but since it is possible for an individual to have a dream he does not understand, we should not be surprised if an artist can have a waking dream he does not understand.

Another recent film which expresses a similar revelation of the unconscious in a highly technologically controlled situation is the Russian science fiction film *Solaris*. The film is fascinating from many points of view, for it shows the soul of "Holy Mother Russia" longing to break out of the iron containers of dialectical materialism. Soviet Russia is laboring under the power of the elite's rational, scientific description of reality. Everything is weighed and measured; every step of history is calibrated in terms of technology, progress, and the spread of Marxism-Leninism to the world and outer space. In the film a group of space scientists are concerned with the problem of a space station. A black and white video tape of an original investigation into the space station is played, and the scientists in the tape pace back and forth like automatons as they question an astronaut who has returned to tell them of things that do not fit into their materialist conceptions of reality. He raves about an ocean on another planet that is alive and communicating with the members of the space station in orbit over the planet, but his obviously emotional reaction to his experience disqualifies him, and the psychologists judge him to have been halucinating.

The years go by and the Solaris controversy sinks into history, and yet the fate of the space station and the men on it is still unresolved. Somehow the controversy will not die, and so the scientists finally resolve to send in an investigator. They choose a psychologist and send him to Solaris alone, but accompanied by all the certainties of his scientific training.

The space station is like a great house of a dying aristocracy before the revolution; the ghosts of the past hang over the place, and the inhabitants do not seem to have the power to move from the past or join the future. But in this great house of outer space, the ghosts literally haunt the place. The space station is in orbit over a great ocean of a distant planet, and it appears that the ocean is alive and trying to communicate with the scientists who remain on the station. The ocean's form of communication is to reach into the soul of each man, find what is missing and unresolved, and return it to him for completion. The ocean is like the law of karma, and each of the scientists is confronted with a ghost from his past. The investigating scientist is sent a double of his wife, who had committed suicide. At first the rational psychologist won't allow himself to believe in the embodied hallucination, and so he finds a way to get rid of her, but each time he rids himself of her, she returns. And with each return, she seems the more real and undeniable; slowly he begins to learn through her about the mystery of human love.

You begin to sense that it is the ocean, too, which is trying to fathom the mystery of human love and is projecting into the space capsule the reflections of the men who have come to colonize it. The reflection is too much for some: one scientist commits suicide; the other wishes to blast the ocean with hydrogen bombs to eliminate the enthralling witch. The astronauts came in search of extraterrestrial life, but when they find it, they cannot deal with it, and instinctively wish to destroy it lest *they* be forced to change. They came as men in machines in search of outer life, but it is their own inner life and the feminine which confronts them. In spite of themselves, they begin to become explorers of the psyche. As they progress in their exploration, the sterile and arrogant concepts of Soviet dialectical materialism begin to recede, and the mysterious life of the ocean becomes more real to them.

The ocean seems to be a planet preparing itself for the evolution of life, and the astronauts from earth seem to be the tiny sperm swimming toward the giant Great Mother of the ovum. But before these humans can impregnate the ocean, they must become clear and more highly conscious of their own natures. As in Jungian psychology, the projections have to be drawn back into the psyche to achieve Unity of Being. The astronauts are encountering their externalized psyches because they are unconscious of their own splits and divisions. As the investigating psychologist encounters the meaning of his love for his wife, he grows stronger until he projects down to the ocean a complete encephalogram of his mind. When he gives completely, the ocean receives completely; the colors of the ocean change, and he becomes free to return home. The homecoming is an archetypal return of the prodigal son of science to the ancient father of Russia. The last scene in the film is a new vision of the nature of home and homecoming in a universe built out of the mystery of love, human and beyond.

Solaris is a fascinating cultural document of the Russian psyche. It speaks volumes about the splits and divisions of the Soviet mind and the intense conflict that is going on between the superficial conscious life of the Soviet Union and the deep wellsprings of the unconscious of "Holy Mother Russia." The materialist elite have constructed a history that is "the lie commonly agreed upon," and all has been rationalized in the stages of progress toward the perfect communist state.

Marx himself, of course, was a visionary who saw history in a grand mythological sweep from primitive communism to a time when "the prehistory of mankind would be at an end," and we would fish in the morning and criticize in the evening; but the institutionalization of Marx in the Leninist-Stalinist state is the negation of Marx's prophetic qualities. Marx wrote in the manner of the prophet Amos, but the Marxists are very much like the sons of Levi whom all the prophets had to denounce. The elite, whether they are priests of the temple or scientists of the state, cannot face the full truth; they can only work to enforce their own rule through the lie commonly agreed upon among themselves. And so release from the tyranny of the elite must come from the places uncontrolled by the conscious ego; the revelations of the larger universe erupt from the unconscious.

Since religion is taboo in the Soviet Union, and since myth is not taken seriously, the only place for religious mythology to surface is in science fiction. *Solaris* should therefore be seen as the equivalent of *2001*. It says much about the cultural convergence of the two technocratic nations that the films are in their *deep structure* so much alike. In each case the ruling class of technocrats cannot accept the nature of the universe, and in each case the journey of the soul involves a homecoming to a new heaven and a new earth. In each case the trick of the movie is to have us look at the familiar with eyes made to wonder once again through art. We ourselves are the creatures from other dimensions who intersected with the primates, and we ourselves live on a planet in which the ocean is alive. If *Solaris* is any indication (and the fact that the version we see has been cut seems to indicate that the Soviets realize its subversive nature), then the Russian consciousness, like one of their winters, is beginning to thaw and the folk soul of the people is beginning to surface. *Solaris,* I hope, is the first crocus of what will be an explosion of spring in Russia.

The persistence of myth in contemporary culture enables us to see that myth does not represent an earlier form, on an evolutionary scale, of a prescientific mentality. Science cannot transcend myth, for myth is basic to science. Myth is an expression of the deep structure of consciousness; it presents not superstitious opinions about gods and natural forces but modalities of the way gods, forces, and humans behave. There are certain thematic configurations of thought in myth which run throughout science, art, and religion, for when you are talking about the archetype of the Great

Mother, you are talking not simply about a neolithic agricultural goddess but about the giant ovum (contrasted to the tiny sperm), the family, and the receptacle of space-time itself.

Once we see the relationship of myth to science, we can see that an Einstein, as much as a Yeats or a Wagner, is a mythopoeic thinker. C. P. Snow has spoken of the two cultures of the humanities and the sciences, but if there are two cultures, they are not the ones he indicates. When I was teaching at MIT, the faculty was told about two patterns of course registration for the students. The engineering majors tended to take all their extra elective courses in the areas of economics and political science; the science majors tended to take their elective courses in arts and the humanities. If there are two cultures, they are not science and the humanities, but Pythagorean and Archimedean forms of knowledge. On the side of the mystery school of Pythagoras are music, poetry, mathematics, and physics; on the side of Archimedes, the first scientist to work for a Department of Defense, are technology, economics, and politics.

The demythologizers in human culture are not the scientists but the Archimedean realists and their admirers. But every time an Archimedean demythologizes an area with the antiseptics of positivism, a Pythagorean physicist comes in to reintroduce the aspect of mystery and cosmological myth. Since the sacred has always to be rescued from the sacerdotal, the demythologizers perform a service to humanity by creating the open secular culture in which a free and joyous resacralization is possible. So whether it is the mystic versus the "God is dead" theologian, or the cosmologist versus the technician, or the prophetic artist versus the fashionable critic, it is a case of exhalation versus inhalation: both are needed.

When you contrast specific areas of expertise with higher

levels of mythopoeic thought, you can see that expertise presents descriptions, prescriptions, and proscriptions, but myth presents a description which is itself a performance of the very reality it seeks to describe. Myth is a form of mathematics which becomes music, not in a structuralist way in which meaning is *reduced* to abstract notation, but in a hieroglyphic way in which the semantic levels of the myth are taken up to a higher, *daimonic* mode of consciousness. Lévi-Strauss has said that "myth is an act of faith in a science yet unborn," but that point of view is still too close to Frazer; it sees myth as a foreshadowing of something which will be truly known through science. You could just as well say that science is an act of faith in a mythology yet unborn, and that when we truly know the universe of which we are a part, we will see that the way DNA spirals in our cells and the way nebulae turn in space are all related to a particular dance of idea and pattern. When a physicist becomes entranced with the symbolic and aesthetic qualities of the quantum theory and begins to see it as a form for contemplation, rather than a problem to be solved in order to make a bigger bomb, then he begins to see that there is a higher level of hieroglyphic knowledge in which art, religion, and science reconverge. Music is the best example of a mode of being in which the description becomes itself the performance of reality.

At the higher levels of knowledge, beyond the dualism of knower and known, there is the pure Being, *Ontos*, which is everything and nothing. For the Buddhist this experience of *sunyata* is described in the chanting of "Form is not different from emptiness, emptiness is not different from form." Ontos is like the divine light which as it comes into space-time breaks down to create the spectrum of vibration from infrared to ultraviolet. At this level of manifestation, Ontos is broken up into the opposites of *physis* and *logos*, matter and mind, but the reflection of Ontos in space-time is neither one nor the other singly, but both in *mythologia*.

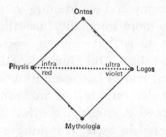

Now the important thing that this *yantra* helps us to see is that mythology is a reflection of being and not simply an expression of the mind's knowing of matter. Another way to put it is that mythology is not a propositional system of knowledge. Truth is not an ideology. Truth is that which overlights the conflict of opposed ideologies, and the conflict of opposed ideologies is what you get in myth: Christ versus Lucifer, Osiris versus Set, Quetzalcoatl versus Tezcatlipoca. On the human level, if capitalist and communist are quarreling with one another, you can't say simply that communism is true and capitalism false. One is arguing for the value of community, the other for the value of individuality, and both are necessary values. The truth overlights both ideologies, and no single human institution or single individual can embody the fullness of truth.

The sage who understood this kind of mythopoeic thought was the physicist Niels Bohr, for it was Bohr who remarked that the opposite of a fact was a falsehood, but that the opposite of one profound truth may well be another profound truth. His hardheaded colleagues wanted to know once and for all whether matter is a wave or a particle, but

Bohr could see beyond the limits of Aristotelian logic to the mythopoeic simultaneity of opposites.

Truth is not a propositional statement; it is a performance: hence the many and maddening variations of a single myth. One of the more rationally unsettling experiences in dealing with a myth is that you can encounter more than one version of the story. Did Quetzalcoatl burn himself on a funeral pyre and rise to become the morning star, or did he sail off to Tlapalan on a raft of snakes? In considering a myth, you are forced to consider the fact that mythology is not simply interested in facts; it is interested in paradoxes, opposites, and transformations—the deep structure of consciousness and not the surface structure of facts and sensory perceptions.

Myth understands that the way Truth and Unity express themselves in life is through the dialectic of opposites. The dialectic can be a violent and tragic conflict for the ignorant, or it can be a compassionate love for the enemy as expressed in the teachings of the Buddha and the Christ. Yeats, as he drew close to his death, moved toward a new understanding of this, a new state of peace after all of the battles of his life.

> It seems to me that I have found what I wanted. When I try to put all into a phrase I say, "Man can embody the truth but he cannot know it." I must embody it in the completion of my life. The abstract is not life and everywhere draws out its contradictions. You can refute Hegel but not the Saint or the Song of Sixpence.[1]

In embodying the Truth, the individual calls his opposite or Shadow into play, and then the dance begins. Then all the areas that he has tried to eliminate from his consciousness begin to be played out. The Sufi leader Pir Vilayat Khan teaches his students to regard all the negativity in their lives as a gift from God, to observe and ask, "What is there in this that returns to me because it comes from me?" Rather than exclaiming, "Oh, my God! Isn't it awful?" the student is taught to observe his fate as karma. Pir Vilayat's meditational technique is similar to *The Tibetan Book of the Dead*, in which the student is counseled to observe the terrifying demons and realize that they are merely the malevolent aspect of beneficent deities. When the student can see the opposites of demon and deity as part of the full play of Truth, he can begin to understand why every myth is constructed around the relationships of life and death, heaven and hell, estrangement and homecoming, hero and monster.

The variations of a single myth, the complex twistings and turnings, are earthquakes that prevent us from settling down and becoming comfortable with easy answers. There is no simple answer which we can put down in our notes and then forget about. The myth requires embodiment, and embodiment requires love, the basic mystery of incarnation. To bring a soul into time requires two, and the embodiment always requires someone other than oneself. You cannot embody the Truth in a narcissistic oneness to say, "Aha! I've got the answer. Now I know what it is all about." The naive ideologue thinks that all he has to do is line up all the good guys on his side and get rid of all the bad guys, and then the Revolution will usher in an era of perfect happiness. But that kind of political, revolutionary thinking is itself a fragment of a myth, and as a fragment it will call its opposite into play, and out of failure and frustration, the revolutionary will be forced to confront the complexity of Truth beyond all ideologies.

If, with a more complex perception than the ideologue's, we see time as the play of opposites, then we can see that history is the performance of myth. When a historian sits down to write, he cannot repeat every fact, and so he is forced to select, and out of the patterns of his selecting emerge the unconscious patterns of myth. When Thucydides described the sailing of the Syracuse expedition, he chose to present the action as a self-proclamation of the power and confidence of the Athenians as they set out to conquer Syracuse. But the deep structure of the scene is Patroklos donning the armor of Achilles in the *Iliad*. Patroklos was warned to observe limits and not to fight beyond the wall, but once he was costumed in the glorious armor of Achilles, he was deceived into thinking he was the hero, and so he went beyond the limit, and was killed. Thucydides was seeing Athenian history through the structures of Homeric myth. The tragedy of history is that the Athenians were not making a mistake; they were simply performing their basic nature. The risk-taking and daring that enabled the small polis to defeat the Persian Empire is the same daring by which the Athenians try to outflank Sparta with an amazing invasion of Syracuse. The daring and risk-taking is Athen's unique excellence, its *arete;* but in the Greek mythological vision of opposites, one's unique excellence and his tragic flaw are one and the same. *Arete* and *hamartia* are one. What raises you up at one moment of time is the same thing that sends you down into the abyss at another. This mysterious power of time to reverse values was understood by Anaximander when he said that things "give justice and make reparation to one another for their injustice, according to the arrangement of Time."

Underlying the superficial movement of historical events is the structure of myth, "the arrangement of Time." Good historians like Thucydides know that the patterns of consciousness in the writing of history derive from literature and myth. It is, therefore, not surprising that Aristotle proclaimed that poetry was superior to history, for poetry presents the universal truth of events and not merely the simple accuracy of facts. The poet thinks at a higher level, at a daimonic level of hieroglyphic thought, and the historian who understands this allows his work to take on the quality of art.

But it is not merely the writing of history that brings myth and symbol into events. In more recent times we can see the play of myth and archetype in the space program. It was by no mere accident that the Russians, limited by their dialectical materialism and technological definitions of culture, chose to send up instruments instead of men into outer space. But we with our cowboy culture needed to show off to the world just what we could do. We had to walk in our space-cowboy boots and ride the range of the moon. Sending up only scientific instruments would have been European sissy stuff. The unconscious compulsion for "Hello, Houston" was Texas in more ways than one.

Whatever the microscopic pattern of expertise may appear to be, when you step back and look at the whole thing, to think big, then you see the mythological nature of the event. This shift in point of view literally took place with several of the astronauts. Russell Schweickart had what can only be called a religious conversion experience when he became the first man to float alone in space and contemplate the earth below.

It is exciting and unsettling when myth and history cross. Whether in the case of Apollo 9, the Paris Commune, or the Easter Rising in Dublin, there is a moment of freedom in which the containment of the ego of the individual and the culture is broken and the longer history of the soul is remembered. For a brief moment we have a sense of other possibilities; at a dramatic turning point on the road of history we come to a place where space-time curves and we can see back to the beginning and forward to the transfiguration of the human race. But it is only a brief instant, for the road turns in again, our vistas collapse, and we return to putting one foot in front of the other on the long march of human evolution.

In the days of the Paris Commune, the Communards shot the hands off the clocks to express the mythical release from time and the prison of history, but there are other ways to take the measure of time than with dead mechanical gadgets. In the great archaic civilizations of Egypt, China, and Mexico, the sages took the measure of time with myth and not machines.

In a sacred, theocratic culture the relationship between myth and history is expressed in the calendar. Before you can have a civilization, before you can have agriculture on scale larger than the neolithic village, you need a calendar. And so in many of the myths the culture hero comes to the villagers and brings with him the gift of the sacred calendar. With the sacred calendar the people can build a community in which the entire universe can take part. When you look at Stonehenge and Avebury in England, Teotihuacán in Mexico, or Machu Picchu in Peru, you are not looking at a simple location; sun and moon and stars enter through the windows as guests. The hitching post of the sun at Machu Picchu hitches the whole community to the solar system. On the vernal equinox at Chichén Itzá in Yucatan, the sun strikes the steps of the great pyramid, el castillo, in such a way that the hard-line edges of the steps cast rounded shadows, and the succession of each curve forms the body of a snake. At the foot of the steps is the head of the plumed serpent, and so the whole staircase becomes, for the few moments of the entry of the earth into spring, the body of the great god Quetzalcoatl. In a theocratic culture, you do not bulldoze a forest to build a shopping plaza; you petition the spirits of the place to build with you a great city to honor the planetary deities. With the divining art of geomancy, you find the right place; with the sacred art of the calendar, you find the right time.

A clock enables you to be on time, but a sacred calendar enables you to move with time; in one, time seems like a monotonous linear series of ticks; in the other, time is a living ocean which extends in all directions. And just as you do not have to move the entire ocean to swim in it, so you do not have to live forever to relate to the cosmic vastness of time. The sacred calendar relates the smallness of the individual life to the greatness of universal time, for it is the calendar which enables the individual to extend his horizons beyond the limits of his ego.

The Maya with their sacred calendar calculated the positions of the stars back in time for millions of years. For some mystical reason we do not understand, the position of certain stars millions of years ago was important to them. They had learned to live with such an extended sense of meaning that time for them wasn't simply the next meal, but the next concert of the stars and the planets. The time of the gods was vast; the time of man was much smaller, but even by our standards their sense of historical time is enormous. For the Long Count of the Maya, human time expresses itself in a 5,124-year cycle; there are 5,124 years of savagery, then 5,124 years of civilization. The period of civilization began for them in 3113 B.C. and will end at midnight on December 24, A.D. 2011. From 1987 to 2011 is the hell period of the calendar, in which earthquakes are prophecied to tear the civilization to pieces. The hell period will be a time of chaos, and at the end of that time, humanity will once again be at the fork of the road, facing a new choice. Humanity can follow its inertial momentum downward into a new period of savagery and dark ages, which will be the easiest thing to do, or it can ascend to a new level in tune with the universe, but not civilized in the traditional definition of the civilizations of the last five thousand years.

The opposites of civilization and savagery pulse back and forth in the waves of the living ocean of time. The civilized people build the cities, and then the barbarians sweep over them. Whether the city is Ur, Rome, or Teotihuacán, the ebb and flow of cultures is much the same. It is easy to envision a scenario for the return of the dark ages for New York, for we need only extrapolate from the morning New York *Times*. Scientists are predicting that we are entering a new cold spell, and that the last few hundred years of industrialization and population growth have been associated with an unusually warm period for the planet. Increased populations will make intense demands for fossil fuel for heating right at the time the oil is needed for petrochemical fertilizers for agriculture, food production, and transportation. We couldn't imagine a worse time for such an event to happen, but the Maya would simply look at their calendar and wonder how we could build a civilization and not even bother to see what time it was.

A scenario for the return of the dark ages is easy to imagine, and a few new books have appeared which have projected such a fate for industrial civilization.[2] But what of the chance to create a culture beyond civilization or savagery? What kind of a culture would that be? Well, if civilization is the problem, then we have to reflect civilization in the mirror of imagination to ask, "What is the mirror-opposite of civilization?" What is the opposite of the division of labor, class stratification, writing, slavery, warfare, etc.? The opposite would be a culture something like that of the dolphins. So let's stretch our imaginations in the direction of the science fiction of John Lilly, accept the fact that the dolphins have a larger brain than we do, and imagine that they have a language. We like to think that our linguistic ability came from the evolutionary sequence of the opposable thumb, tool production, and gestures; but how did the dolphins arrive at their position if they do not produce tools and lack the great opposable thumb? The sociobiologist E. O. Wilson claims, "In intelligence the bottle-nosed dolphin probably lies somewhere between the dog and the rhesus monkey,"[3] but for the sake of stretching our imaginations, let us accept the views of Dr. Lilly and see the dolphins as being as intelligent as, or even more intelligent than, we are. Rousseau had his noble savage, Jonathan Swift had his Houyhnhnm, and Dr. Lilly has his dolphin; in each case the critic of civilization has imagination enough to realize that from a truly broad point of view, civilization may not be really worth it. If we accept Freud's point of view that civilization is based on repression and generates the neurosis of mankind, then the dolphin's polymorphously perverse life of erotic play could be a culture perhaps even more advanced than that of Professor Wilson's Harvard.

Even without the benefit of Esalen hot baths, the dolphins swim naked in the tropical sea, and do not have to wait for the females to go into estrus to enjoy sexuality. Like humans, but unlike the chimpanzee, the dolphin has eroticized time to eliminate estrus in the females. With full sexuality and linguistic ability, the dolphins have what most of the old creation myths point out to be the significant endowments of human nature. And if they lack Las Vegas, the World Trade Center, and the hydrogen bomb, perhaps they have found an evolutionary short cut and have eliminated the detour of civilization altogether. William Blake said, "Energy is eternal delight"; so let us imagine the dolphins swimming in the erotic delight of the energy of the sea, and communicating back and forth to one another in a multidimensional "Bead Game" that is the best of music and mathematics, and then some. Then let us go on to imagine that the most elegant of their creations is beamed to the Andromeda Galaxy, and through the warps in space, they hear Andromeda suggest another theme and variation. If we imagine that the dolphins can hear the music of the spheres, and that their larger brains have evolved for that purpose, then perhaps we can understand why they do not, like our astronauts, have to get their rocks off the moon.

Of course, all of this is just an exercise in science fiction, but if we can tolerate even a little stretching of our imaginations, we can begin to see that what we take for granted as the advanced achievements of a progressive civilization are primitive by other standards. The leviathan and behemoth of the World Trade Center is really vulgar and nouveau riche, a competition of New York with Houston and Chicago to see who can make the most absurdly energy-intensive structures in the world. High above the tenements of Harlem and the depths of the sea, the industrial managers can sit in Windows on the World and discuss the GNP. If our civilization had a memory equivalent to that of the Maya, it could recall the crashing towers of Atlantis, but our sense of time is short and when we look to the future we turn our backs on the past. Perhaps that is why in a neurotic repetition compulsion, we keep on recreating the old tragedy in a new context.

According to more ancient notions, the more highly conscious a culture is, the greater its horizon of time and the stronger its memory. If we go back to Plato and his four types of men in the *Republic*, the appetitive, the spirited, the rational, and the daimonic, we can see that each type has an associated horizon of time. The man of appetites, the man of the body, is locked into the time span of his stomach. If his stomach is full, he snores off to sleep, happy in the summer sun. His span of time is but a few hours, and he is not concerned with amassing wealth or achieving glory. He plays Falstaff to Prince Hal. He's not concerned about conquering France; he's for taverns and wenching.

The spirited man is, by contrast, concerned with glory. He is the prince, the samurai, the warrior, the athlete. Concerned with *arete*, with excellence, the spirited man has a time span not determined by his stomach but by his glory, his power, his fame. The time span is of years, not hours. But a warrior, an athlete, or a gunfighter can only be in his glory for a handful of years; sooner or later a younger and greater opponent will come to take his fame away, and all his glory goes to dust. The story of the spirited man is a phallic myth of rise and fall; it is the story of all the old heroes, Hektor, Achilles, or even the older corn gods of the Near East, Tammuz and Dumuzi.

Since muscle cannot triumph more than a decade or two at the most, there are those who prefer to depend on their knowledge. The rational man has seen the heroes come and go, and he waits his time, for he is conscious of time not just in hours or years but in millennia. The rational man can relate the life of his culture to that of other cultures and other civilizations. The rational man is the archetype for all our educational systems; he is the scientist, the scholar, the educated businessman, the statesman.

With each move from appetitive to spirited to rational, we have taken a jump in orders of magnitude of time, from hours to years to millennia. If we move beyond the rational man to the daimonic man, the man of the soul, the sage, we move from millennia to millions of years. Such a move is the difference in consciousness of the hero, Gilgamesh, and the sage, Utnapishtim; it is the difference between ourselves and the Mayan astronomers who calculated star positions back millions of years. The man of the soul such as Sri Aurobindo thinks in terms of the entire span of evolution, and even beyond to the timeless realm of eternity, before and after the soul's evolution in the physical universe. But because the daimonic man, the sage, can see the entire panorama of time, he can understand how the microcosm fits into the pattern of the macrocosm, and this understanding, and not mere prediction, is the nature of prophecy. The 5,124-year Long Count cycle of the Maya is simply one unit in a larger period, but we who are inside this cycle cannot see outside it; therefore, we think that all history is contained within this single unit. We are like ants crawling across Picasso's "Guernica"; we can sense a succession of changes, but we cannot see the whole painting.

The ancient Maya, whether through religious revelation, intuition, or the detritus of a lost civilization's science, could see the whole picture. They could see a periodicity to the civilizational cycle. To dream up a science fiction answer to the question of how they came up with the Long Count, I imagine that there was a missing civilization, and that this civilization knew something about the life of the sun that we don't. I also imagine that the heavy emphasis on the sun in the religions of Mexico and Egypt derived from this lost, previous civilization. I imagine then that every 5,124 years or so, something happens in the sun, and that this pulse in the solar wind greatly affects our weather, and possibly even the magnetic envelope of the earth, and the stability of the tectonic plates. The bible of the Maya, the *Popul Vuh,* as well as the Indian *Rig-Veda,* expresses a time of wandering of the tribes during great catastrophes; I am assuming that there is some basis in history for the mythologies of cosmic disasters. I do not entirely accept the theories of Dr. Velikovsky; I think the *structure* of his theory of catastrophism is right, but the *surface content* is wrong. The *Rig-Veda,* the *Popul Vuh,* the *Gilgamesh* epic all speak of catastrophes in the past that have wiped out civilizations, so I assume that there is something to the story. But the Maya calculated time forwards as well as backwards, and their date of A.D. 2011 is the prophesied end of an epoch. Once again I dream that as we approach the end of the 5,124-year cycle, all hell is about to break loose in the sun. Perhaps the scientists who have noticed changes in the earth's magnetic field, as well as changes in the weather, have seen the early warning signals for our own culture. At all events, if there is something to Mayan astrophysics more than mere superstition and witchcraft, we will find that our civilization is not as strong as we thought. Our fragile, overextended postindustrial civilization will find it difficult to hold together, and our materialistic and arrogant world view may prove to be inappropriate to the new solar conditions.

If you don't like the science fiction mythology I am spinning out, then take the myth simply as a metaphor for the Marxist internal contradictions of our civilization. When we come to the fork in the road between now and A.D. 2011, we either have to take the easy way out to roll downhill into savagery, or make the quantum leap into a new level of cultural evolution beyond civilization and savagery. Just such a level is what I have in mind when I speak about "planetary culture." As a primitive Celtic animist still lingering on in the modern industrial world, I am in accord with Giordano Bruno and Pythagoras and feel that the sun is alive and is the body of what the Buddhists like to call "a sentient being." I see the sun as both star and archangel of evolution in our world system and I assume that He-She is forcing us into this fix so that our evolution can keep moving. I also imagine that the sun did something similar eons ago when the forests began to shrink, the savannas open out, and the volcanoes explode, as early *Homo* wandered out from the forests into the open, where the fragile creatures bent down to pick up rocks and stammer at one another in stark amazement at the fierce, unforested sun.

As you can see, I don't think that the major steps in human evolution have been taken because humans wanted to take them, and I don't think that the next step will be taken through the conscious manipulations of genetic engineering and recombinant DNA. I assume that the weather and the reversal of the earth's magnetic field are beyond the management of human science, and I further assume that just such occasions of what the scientists would call "chance" are what control the evolution of life. The atheist sees a brutish and impersonal Chance; the animist sees the terrifying and beautiful archangel of evolution; but both would agree that the polite and watered-down visions of homey comfort provided by the clergy of organized religion and the psychotherapists of the human-potential movement have little sense of the universe we are in.

The transition from civilization to planetization is a turn on the spiral which brings us perilously close to a return to savagery. The actions of the next thirty years will determine whether we make the transition or start from scratch again to try to approach the universe with something other than an arrogant industrial civilization. The image for the turning of the spiral is the ancient myth I mentioned earlier of the Ouroboros, the serpent which bites its tail to release the poison that is the antidote to its own illness. To a scientific and rational mentality, mythopoeic thought seems to be a superstitious poison, but for our culture as a whole, the apparent poison is the antidote to the disease of industrial civilization.

It is from deep impulses in the collective unconscious that our contemporary culture has gone back to archaic forms of thought in Yoga, Tibetan Buddhism, Sufism, Celtic animism, geomancy, and Chinese medicine, for implicit in these forms of knowledge is another world view, a world view in which consciousness is continuous with matter. The great divorce of consciousness from matter, of feeling from thinking, of science from art and religion is not characteristic of the archaic world view. The planetization of the archaic, the Hegelian *Aufheben* of the mystical by the modern, is the stage of growth our world culture is now entering. In the sacred marriage of mysticism and science, the Pythagorean unity of opposites will engender a new world culture beyond the mysticism of the East or the materialism of the West.

It is important to realize that this new world culture is not a return to the past. In the Renaissance, the great prince of Florence Cosimo de' Medici and the Platonic scholar Gemistus Plethon were fascinated by the ancient Orphic and Pythagorean mystery schools of archaic Greece. With the help of de' Medici and Plethon, Marsilio Ficino tried to reawaken an interest in the Hermetic tradition in the Florentine Academy, but the effect of the Academy on the scholars in Europe was not to go back in time, but forward into the Renaissance and the dawn of the modern world. The injection of Hermetic mysticism into the dogmatic slumbers of the Latin Church helped to awaken Europe and create a wholly new consciousness. In a similar way, I would argue, the injection of the great mystical schools of the past is helping to awaken us from the dogmatic slumber of industrial materialism, capitalist, and communist.

In the gyres within gyres, modern culture is going back where it started in the Renaissance, but the entire Western civilization is going back where it started in the urban revolution of ancient Sumer. (Yeats has explained in *A Vision* how these gyres within gyres turn, and how all the spirals can line up.) As we turn, we recapitulate and reconstitute certain earlier situations, but we do not literally return to the same place, for now we have the consciousness of all that has come in between. So it is very important to realize that we are not going back to Yoga, Sufism, and Tibetan

Buddhism; we are going forward to a new age of spirituality, in which there will, most likely, be a resacralization of life but no religions as we have known them in the period of civilization. The young people of today who take on Arabic names or sprout turbans on their heads or eat nothing but brown rice and miso soup are not the wave of the future; they are simply children at play with cultures. They are no different from the Singhalese teenagers I heard in Colombo who were singing country-western songs in an artificial southern twang.

Perhaps the best way to get perspective on the contemporary scene is to step out of science *and* the esoteric schools of thought to see how both are situated in the larger historical landscape. (This is pretty much what we try to do at Lindisfarne.) If we consider geology *and* mysticism and remember Gloucester's line from *King Lear* that "these late eclipses in the sun and moon portend no good to us," we can smile as modern geology talks about the relationship of the lunar eclipse to the Anchorage earthquake. If in 1982, when all the planets line up on the other side of the sun and pull on the earth's tectonic plates, there are more earthquakes, modern geology will come to a new appreciation of ancient mythopoeic forms of thought.

This reconvergence of geology and mythology is not unique to one branch of science but is taking place in all fields of knowledge. In physiology we can see a relationship between myth and science in the work of Paul McLean on "the three brains of man."[4] Dr. McLean points out that man has a spinal brain (the ancient reptilian brain), the limbic cortex (the mammalian brain of emotion, of flight or fight), and the neocortex (the cerebral hemispheres of the higher rational functions). Now this modern approach is an interesting way to come at the functioning of the nervous system in esoteric practices of illumination. In ancient theocratic cultures, sacred knowledge was expressed in hieroglyphs, not in abstract concepts. The hieroglyph for the three brains in ancient Mexico, for example, is the plumed serpent. The snake makes its way up from the earth, coiling around the trunk, until at the top of the tree it turns into a bird and flies into the higher dimensions. The ancient city of Teotihuacán, the city of the plumed serpent, Quetzalcoatl, was the place where "the serpent learns to fly."[5] In Yucatan and Guatemala, the magical quetzal birds, whose feathers were so treasured, lived only at the tops of the trees in the sunlight. In the jungle the tree was rooted in darkness, but at the top, opening toward the light of the sun was the great bird. In the same way, human consciousness was rooted in instinct and matter, the residuum of evolution still contained in the subconscious mind; but through human growth a level of passionate awareness had arisen. The higher consciousness, however, was beyond the passions and made its nest at the top of the brain in the full light of the illuminating sun. In India this relationship of the subconscious mind and the superconscious was expressed in the hieroglyph of the lotus, which has its roots in the mud, its spinal stem in the water, but its petals opening in the air toward the light. What is expressed in these hieroglyphs of plumed serpent and lotus is a compressed dissertation on the evolution of the human central nervous system. The evolution of the brain, however, is not simply a record of the past but a continuing process into the future. The path of initiation is a miniaturization and recapitulation of the entire evolutionary saga of the soul's movement through space-time. Ontogeny recapitulates phylogeny, and before we can go on to the next level of evolution, we must go over in full consciousness the places we have traveled in unconsciousness.

Now what is the knowledge of the three human brains doing in ancient Mexico? Did the Mexicans discover the relationship between initiation and the evolution of the central nervous system because human nature is true to form the world around? Do all cultures discover independently the same material over and over again? Or did this knowledge come to Mexico by diffusion from Egypt, or India, or China; or did all of these cultures derive from an earlier Atlantis? There are no answers, only theories and groups forming around one theory or another. In our culture now, myth and science are in opposite camps, and if you give allegiance to one, you gain enemies in the other. If you give allegiance to both myth and science, as I do, then you end up by having enemies and friends in both camps.

This polarization between myth and science today, I believe, is only temporary. As with inhalation and exhalation, the two functions must come together if there is to be life. If you work in a laboratory and dissect cadavers, you will gain one kind of knowledge about the structure of the central nervous system. If you practice the yoga of Quetzalcoatl, you can possibly experience higher states of consciousness and illumination. In our society you have to choose one over the other, but after the planetization of the archaic has been completed as a historical process in new forms of education, a scientific knowledge of physiology and a personal experience of yoga will take place in the same individual.

If we shift from a consideration of physiology to botany, we can see another relationship between myth and science in the best-seller *The Secret Life of Plants*. If plants are alive and responsive to human consciousness, then what the community of Findhorn is playing out for the modern Western world is the return of animism to a technological society. But animism need not be restricted to plants, for if you consider the "Gaia Hypothesis" of Lovelock and Margolis,[6] that the earth's atmosphere is not simply a gaseous fluid into which substances are dumped by animals, plants, and factories, but the metabolism of a complex organism, then we have the extended animism we encountered in the living ocean of *Solaris.*

The notion that the earth is a living being is an ancient one. In the Taoist science of ancient China, geomancy or *feng-shui,* subtle forces were said to flow through the earth in ways analogous to the circulation of the blood in humans. To build a city, the Chinese believed that you could not simply level the trees; you had to consult the landscape, chart the flow of the *ch'i* force, the balance of yin and yang, and then place the homes, trees, and rocks with utmost care in a pattern of universal harmony. A city which was not so planned was a parasitical growth, a cancerous tumor on the earth. Once we have relearned the wisdom of *feng-shui,* I assume that the smaller, symbiotic cities of the future will be healthier places than New York and Calcutta. And once again, I assume that if we complete the perilous rite of passage from civilization to planetization, the future education of city planners will include *feng-shui,* the essays of D. H. Lawrence, and the poetry of Wordsworth.

Once the ground has been prepared for cities and villages through the arts of geomancy, ancient and modern, then mythopoeic thought can extend itself into the field of architecture. The architecture of the future, I imagine, will be modeled on the architecture of matter itself, seen not in its aggregate nature as plastic material to be molded into shape, but in its musical structure as a crystal or as an archetypal geometrical form. The acoustical space of the ancient pyramids, cathedrals, and mosques is a celebration of sacred geometry. The shape of the church gives back to the chanter a shape to the reverberations of his psalm. If architecture has been said to be "frozen music," then music can be said to be moving crystals. The chant that echoes in the cathedral or mosque is an echo of geometrical structure as well as of physical sound. Sacred geometry is a vision of divine intelligence, the logos, revealing itself in all forms, from the logarithmic spiral of a seashell to the hexagonal patterns of cooling basalt, from the architecture of the molecule to the galaxy.

At Lindisfarne we had a course on "Cosmology and the Geometry of Sacred Architecture" conducted by Robert Lawlor. The course was an exploration of the theories of the Egyptologist Schwaller de Lubicz. Our work in this area has been similar to the work of Keith Critchlow and the London group Research into Lost Knowledge.[7] But whether we are studying the Temple of Luxor with Schwaller de Lubicz or Chartres and Glastonbury Abbey with Keith Critchlow, we are seeing a vision in which geometry itself had a direct effect on the human body and mind.

Now if you stop to consider the relationship of mythopoeic forms of thought to all these different sciences: architecture, city-planning, biology, and geology, you can see a new pattern emerging, a pattern which is really a new world view. The universe is not a black box containing floating bits of junk left over from the "big bang" explosion; it is a consciousness-saturated solution. Mind is not simply located in the human skull; animal, vegetable, and mineral forms are all alive. Just as ice, steam, and water are all different forms of H_2O, and dreamless sleep, dreaming, and waking are all different forms of consciousness, so animal, vegetable, and mineral are all simply different states of divine consciousness. Our smaller minds have been used to abstract the organism from the environment, to abstract mind from the body, to abstract culture from nature; and thus we have created the peculiar pathology of industrial civilization. Gregory Bateson argues that to avert a total ecological catastrophe we must begin to think about ourselves in nature in a new way: the organism *plus* the environment must be seen as the basic unit of evolution.[8]

If the organism and the environment can come together in sympathetic resonance, then we will see in the near future a new instinctive technology, a new symbiotic architecture, new metaindustrial villages, and a resacralization of knowledge in which science and mysticism converge. In this resacralization I do not believe we will see the rise of one single universal religion; rather, the attempt to collectivize the planet under one global sect will be demonic, the Antichrist, the ape of God. I believe the future will bring the spring thaw, the melting of the rigid ice of the Church into the living waters of a new sacred way of life. We will move closer to the sacred way of life of hunters and gatherers than to the temple religions of civilization.

Perhaps the best way for me to describe the re-creation of the past in the future is to follow Plato's example again to tell "a likely story."

Once upon a time, a very long time ago, there were two brothers. One was big and strong and highly respected as a great warrior; the other was looked upon with scorn, for he was soft, gentle, and effeminately given to lying among the flowers to play his flute as he gazed into the sky. A time came when the town of the brothers set about the work of constructing a great temple to honor their gods. Since the oldest brother was the largest and strongest man in the community, the elders asked him to move the huge stones needed to make a truly holy temple, after the fashion of the ancients. The older brother responded with muscle, but he could not move even the smallest of the large rocks the priests wanted. So then in good warrior fashion, he set about organizing the conquered slaves in work gangs; but no matter how hard he beat them with the whip, the slaves could not budge the stones. While the slaves and the older brother were struggling with great effort, the younger brother came strolling in from his morning with the flowers and the sky. He looked at the people and the stones, and then he looked *into* the stones and recognized them, for he could see their names. With a smile he took out his flute and began to play. The older brother shouted that this was no time to play, that there was real work for real men to do, but his shouts were stopped by an exclamation from the slaves, for the great stones were beginning to sway back and forth in rhythm with the music of the younger brother's flute. Stopping for a moment, the young brother told the priests that they should speak to the stones and tell them that they were being moved to make a great temple to honor the gods. And when the priests had done this, the young brother told the slaves to take the stones gently by the hand, for they were very, very old, and lead them along the path to the site of the temple. And then he began to play his flute again. The stones began to sway back and forth; and as they did, the slaves gently guided them and the great stones danced themselves down the road into the place the priests had chosen for them.

Contained in this variation on an old legend is a racial memory of a lost technology. If we look around the world from Baalbek in Lebanon to Angkor Wat in Cambodia to Easter Island or to Sacsahuamán in Peru or Newgrange in Ireland and Stonehenge in England, we see a culture or cultures which built sacred structures out of huge stones. According to D. H. Lawrence, or more recently John Michell,[9] the archaic cultures are really expressions of a single global culture which had a high magical science. All our legends of magic and wizards are simply memories of the days of this lost sacred science. From the point of view of this ancient knowledge, matter was alive and was singing; if you knew its key signature cabbalistically, you could vibrate in resonance with it, and dance the rocks into place. To hear the music of matter, however, took long years of training and meditation.

The memory of this lost knowledge has lingered on in myths around the world—in the myths of Orpheus in Greece, Väinämöinen in Finland, and Sotuknang in the land of the Hopi. The myth is a vision of a science which is the mirror-opposite of industrial technology. We will need this mirror image if we are going to reflect on ourselves as we consider ways to pass through the planetary rite of passage.

All the archaic images are surfacing out of the collective unconscious. The ancient ways and ancient esoteric schools have taken on a new life even in the midst of a technological society. From Tibet, from the Middle East, from Scotland, from Mexico, and from the American Southwest, the archaic ways are coming back and offering themselves to us. They have lived in secret for a long time, and in secrecy they have flourished. Now, as they blaze forth into the open, they will die and, in their death, make a new life possible. Like a dying star that in its explosive end scatters the material needed for the evolution of life, the supernova of the esoteric and the occult we are witnessing is both an end and a beginning.

The beginning is in our midst, for black Africa, yellow Asia, red America, and white Europe have come together on this continent. The culture of America has become the alchemical crucible in which the evolutionary transformation of humanity is all about us.

FOUR

THE
FUTURE
OF
KNOWLEDGE

WHEN A PROFESSIONAL FUTUROLOGIST tries to write
about the future, he usually ends up by writing about
the present, but when I set myself the task of trying to
imagine the future, I find myself drawn back to images of a
remote and mythic past. Perhaps because I am a cultural
historian, my orientation to both present and future is from
images of the past, but I also like to think that it is because
the mystery of the future has its roots in the myths of the
past.

All our actions are future-oriented, for it is the consciousness of the future we carry inside us that determines
our immediate actions in the present. If we do one thing, it
is because we expect another, and that expectation, of
course, comes from the past. We carry time around with us,
and the way in which time is made portable is through the
use of images. It is the mythic image of time past, or time
future, which makes us conscious in our uniquely human
way, whether we are Plato's appetitive, spirited, rational, or
daimonic man. The type of human beings we are simply sets
the limit on the length of time we can carry in our minds—
hours, years, millennia, or the eons of cosmic duration.

Each of Plato's four types of man is limited by an external

span of time, but each is also defined by an internal dynamic of limitation. The limit to the appetitive mode of being is expressed in the dynamic of frustration and satisfaction. One longs for something, and then the satisfaction of that appetite destroys the appetite itself so that one can relax into a drunken sleep. The decadent Romans became somewhat sophisticated in the nature of appetites, and they tried to push beyond the limit by vomiting up their food at great banquets so that they could continue feasting to their mind's content. When the mind intensifies a basic drive or appetite, it is no longer a question of merely satisfying the needs of the body but of satisfying the passions.

When we move from the appetitive man to the spirited man, the man of passion, we move to appetites that take more time to be satisfied. You can satisfy your hunger or thirst in a moment, but if you have a passion for money, fame, conquest, or the love of a beautiful but remote woman or man, then years may be consumed in the burning of that passion. But as in the world of appetites, the consummation of a passion is the destruction of that passion.

Although the passions may take more time to be satisfied, they are still like the appetites in that their internal dynamic is one of frustration and satisfaction, tension and release, motion and rest. The world of the passions is a world of conflict, and the ultimate passion is for rest from the conflict, release from the agony of desire. But even in the passion to be free of the passions, we play out a dynamic of opposites. When we are in the middle of conflict, we imagine a pastoral of complete peace and freedom. In one of his poems Yeats imagines a lake isle of pastoral tranquillity and says to himself, "I will arise and go now, and go to Innisfree." The poem came to Yeats as he was walking down the Strand in London; he saw a water-jet in a shop window and his mind was set to thinking of the light and water in his native Sligo.

In the midst of London he remembers the West of Ireland, but the great poet of European civilization was not the hermit of Innisfree but a frequenter of the salons of Paris, the town houses in London, and the great estates of the English aristocracy. Pastoral worlds are imaginary places, and whenever we try to move into them to take up permanent residence, we find ourselves bored and restless and thinking of London, Paris, and New York. In New York City we think of living on an island in Maine; on the island in Maine we think of the excitement of the city. After a short period of rest, we long again for motion, and the peace of the country seems vacuous when compared to the civilizational excitement and complexity of the city. The human compromise of the rich has been to come to terms with the contradiction by living in both places during the year.

Summer home and winter home may seem to be casual expressions of human passions, but the conflict can be raised to a more archetypal level if you think about the theme of wandering and homecoming in Western literature. All the time that Odysseus is seeing the wonders of the world, he is thinking of his Penelope back home, but as the other legends have it, when he does come home, he cannot rest and once again sets out for unknown wanderings toward his final rest in death. Even in achieving his intensely desired homecoming, Odysseus cannot rest forever, for that kind of permanent rest only makes home into a tomb.

Human beings are never satisfied, and all our literature simply shows that when we have one thing, we desire another. The beautiful woman wants to be ugly so that she will not be bothered by men; the ugly woman wants to be beautiful so that she can be pursued. The married man chases after women and dreams of a harem; once divorced, he grows tired of his harem, and dreams of having a single queenly wife. Like the tick of a clock or the beating of the heart, human life swings back and forth between the opposites of frustration and satisfaction, motion and rest.

When we move from the world of the passions to the world of the mind, from Plato's spirited man to the rational, the dialectical nature of the dynamic of frustration and satisfaction takes on a new life. We long for a complete and total explanation. We long for a science that is absolute and perfect, in which each law interlocks with every other law to form one complete, all-embracing mechanical system. Professor Marvin Minsky at MIT, one of the world's leading experts on computers and artificial intelligence, has indicated his contempt for the sloppy passions of irrational human beings by working to perfect intelligence in machines. Expressing disdain for the so-called superiority of the human brain, he has exclaimed, "What is the brain but a computer made out of meat?" If we could only hook up the brain to a computer, then we could really begin to live. For Professor Minsky the future of knowledge is simply the increasing replacement of biological processes with artificial and cultural ones. We replace the earth with a space colony, and then replace the inhabitants' minds with computers, until finally an absolute, stainless-steel perfection is reached.

As you can see, Professor Minsky's dream of artificial intelligence is a pastoral; it is a dreamworld free of conflict, a place of complete rest and death. The poet Yeats dreams of a pastoral world which is completely natural; the scientist Minsky dreams of one which is completely artificial. But neither pastoral is truly human, for culture is neither completely natural nor completely artificial; culture is the relationship between those opposites. The relationship between the opposites is the interface, the place of life, transformation, and evolution.

The desire to achieve a completely artificial intelligence, whether through the cybernetics of Minsky or the behavioral engineering of Skinner, is the desire to escape motion and conflict in the rest of a complete system. But when we do elaborate an explanation, we become bored and long to be released again from our perfected systems. The total explanation becomes totalitarian, and we look for release through revolutionary energies and impulses. It may take a culture a few centuries to become bored with the explanations of a Thomas Aquinas or a Karl Marx, but sooner or later the revolutionary impulse will arise to challenge the system, and Orc will come forth to challenge Urizen.

But there is another kind of limit which is built into the way in which the mind constructs reality. There is a limit inherent in the nature of explanation itself. Every description tries to be complete, but by the very nature of a description, it cannot be total. A description is a limited thing; it is the map and not the territory. A description can only work because it is not the whole, and so it is a form of vision through blindness.

There is a limit to the power of description and explanation. As Heisenberg has expressed it in the indeterminacy principle, if you know an elementary particle's location, you cannot know its momentum; if you know its momentum, you cannot know its location. The indeterminacy principle upset Einstein, for he was looking for a total unified field theory; he could not believe that God played dice with the universe, and so he tried to push beyond the limit to achieve the mind of God, to know the universe as God must know it. He saw Heisenberg as irreligious and could not see that the indeterminacy principle is a gift from God to us, the gift of our freedom. The universe is not a complex machine but a relationship between freedom and order. The rage for order of men and godlings is a drive to determine events through secret knowledge, but God has arranged a more public and universal demonstration of freedom in the limits of science.

Another expression of the limits to scientific description is in mathematics in Gödel's theorem. Gödel has shown that no description can be logically self-contained and total; mystery is always leaking in; the mathematician is always having to assume or refer to things outside his system. Whether it is a theorem, an atom, or an ecosystem, nothing in nature is closed and self-contained; energies from other orders are always moving across our self-created boundaries. If you consider the import of Heisenberg's indeterminacy principle and Gödel's theorem, you can see that both express the limits of a description.

Heisenberg has said that we do not have a science of nature but a science of man's knowledge about nature. In the quantum theory, simple, naive materialism disappears and we begin to discover, in the words of Castaneda's Don Juan, that we do not live in reality but in a description of reality. The project for the sorcerer is "to stop the world," peer around the corners of the cultural description of reality to encounter being in its fullness. The sorcerer can see the description as mere figure against the ground of being, and can, therefore, accept the limitations of all descriptions. But the scientist wants his description to be complete and all-embracing; he wants the figure to be coextensive with the ground. Such an overextension would, of course, annihilate the edges of the figure to dissolve in it pure being, and science itself as a cultural reality would be dissolved into mysticism. The ultimate enantiodromia would be achieved: science in trying to eradicate mysticism in a total extension of its power in all directions would dissolve into a universal mysticism. Whether we wish to see contemporary physics as the resolution or the dissolution of science depends on our point of view, but the transformation of physics from materialism into process modes of consciousness has already taken place.

Whether we approach experience as a physicist or as a sorcerer, *being* is always frustrating *knowing*, frustrating our attempts to control reality, shattering our desires to hold the world in a tight scientific grip. The scientist, like the archetypal magician Faust, is always striving, always in pursuit of one total explanation, but after he achieves a theory, the very forces that created it, finish it, and he or his successor is left to start all over again.

So whether you are talking about the appetitive, the spirited, or the rational man, you are still talking about the basic dynamic of frustration and satisfaction, tension and release, motion and rest. The shock of incarnation startles the soul; suddenly it finds itself in a body of space-time, and whether it rattles the cage of its skin as a glutton, an athlete, a scientist, or a sorcerer, it beats at the cage in tension and release, motion and rest.

If we look at this dialectical pulse of experience through historical time, we can see that there is also a historical dynamic of the motion and rest of ideas. An idea begins as a vision in an individual and then becomes an institution. The movement from charismatic idea to routine institution has been chronicled in the sociology of Max Weber, but the movement is simply another modern application of the ancient notion of the enantiodromia. We begin with the Sermon on the Mount and end up with the Inquisition. We begin with Pythagoras's school at Crotona and end up with the educational bureaucracies of the modern world. Thus we encounter another limit: for an idea to survive, it must become organized, but the organization of an idea brings about a loss of energy and vision which begins to kill the original idea. Culture is a process in which every idea, if it is to survive the inventor, must be slowly killed.

No embodiment of an idea in an institution can be complete: if you know an idea's visionary momentum, you cannot know its societal location; if you can locate the idea, then you have lost sense of its visionary momentum. As you develop an idea into its complete realization, by the time it has become realized, it has turned into its exact opposite. The Church cannot be Jesus Christ; the Communist party cannot be Karl Marx. The way a society disguises this movement away from the original vision is in idolizing the founder. To disguise the perversion of Gandhi's principles, modern India celebrates him with great show; now as China prepares to abandon the thought of Mao, it will create an apotheosis of him to cover the desecration.

Depressing as all of this is, it still is possible to see that the historical limits we keep bumping up against are divine gifts. A landscape is not a cage; we do not have to smash into a mountain or drive off a cliff to appreciate the scenery. The limits to description or institutionalization rescue us from our totalizing instincts. Rescued from the closed systems of completeness, we are given the gifts of openness and freedom, and this essential freedom is our patrimony, a gift from God the Father. In our ignorance, we would lock ourselves in, into our appetites, or our churches, or our scientific theories, for we always want more than we need. But the daimon is always there to whisper in our ear to be careful for what we pray, for we will get it. We want something out of ignorance, and then when it comes to us, it seems the exact opposite, and we are horrified at the reflection of our own desires in action.

After a depressing period of watching the enantiodromias of history swing back and forth, or after a period of frustration, watching all the mathematical and scientific descriptions crash up against their limits, one begins to be aware that he has been *observing* the limits of the mind. What is this other consciousness that can observe the mind? Without knowing it, we have suddenly stumbled into another level of awareness, in which everything is reversed. Before, every event was figure against the ground of our own personality; now we ourselves become figure against the ground of another being. Who is this creature who uses me as I use my hand?

It is the daimon. At the rational level of experience, the world is split into twos: light and dark, male and female, one and zero, good and evil. The daimonic consciousness, however, is the consciousness of the opposites seen together. In our normal binocular vision, we look out the right eye and see the comedy, and out of the left eye to see the tragedy, but the daimonic consciousness looks out through the third eye.

The opening of the third eye can come through meditation, for when you contemplate the relationship between motion and rest, sorrow and joy, form and emptiness, you begin to observe the simultaneity of the opposites; and then as you move beyond rational theology or ideology, you can begin to think mythically to see the relationship between Christ and Lucifer, Osiris and Set, Quetzalcoatl and Tezcatlipoca.

The way in which the daimonic consciousness has been presented in culture has been through myth, legend, and fairy tale, but because we have been raised to think in terms of ideology, be it Sunday-school religion or Marxist propaganda, we tend to identify with only one character in the story, the good guy. But the story is about the relationship between the good guy and the bad guy. Consider the myth of Set and Osiris. Now we all know that Set is the bad guy and Osiris is the good guy, but let's look again. Set is out to get Osiris, and so he builds a coffin, tailor-made to Osiris's measurements, and then he throws a party to show off the coffin to his friends. Just for a lark, he invites his guests to try it on. It's all great sport, and the guests enjoy getting in and out of the coffin. Finally, it's Osiris's turn. He gets in, the coffin fits perfectly, but before he can get out, Set slams the lid down on him, nails it down with glee, and flings it into the river.

The coffin is the body. Osiris had been winging it in the Empyrean, free and undeterminate, but at an evolutionary steady-state. Set locks the soul into the body and flings it into the river of time, and so sets the whole cycle of human evolution going. If you want to look at the story from Set's point of view, he is the hero; but, of course, that is simply to swing from one point of view to another and not to look at the whole.

Osiris, like the soul or the daimon, is unlimited, and that is the source of his limitation. In Yeats's *A Vision* the daimon is described as an undifferentiated sphere outside space and time and unable to communicate directly with other souls. To those unfamiliar with Yeats, I would suggest associating the *daimon* with what is called "the causal body" in theosophy. For those more familiar with traditional, academic philosophy, Yeats's daimon, as an undifferentiated sphere isolated from other phenomena, can be compared with "the windowless monads" in the metaphysics of Leibniz. The daimons glide by one another as perfect spheres enjoying a circular solitude. Because there is no extension, there is no connection; they have to project into space-time to gain experience, experience of determination and limitation. Once more, think of the film 2001 as a variant of Gnostic myths of the Fall. The beings beyond space-time take up the body of the man-apes. Whether they take up the body willingly, or are locked into it as Osiris was, the condition of incarnation becomes the same.

The projection of the daimon into space-time is the ego. Arising out of the condition of the unlimited comes the principle of limitation, the mystery of the Word becoming flesh.

In order to achieve experience, the soul creates a vehicle, but the vehicle, because it is, by desire and definition, limited, cannot remember the soul. Just as we find it difficult to remember our dreams upon waking, so do we find it difficult to remember the daimon upon waking into incarnation. You could say that all the meditative paths of the great universal religions are simply techniques to help us recall who we are and where we come from.

Or think of it this way. Imagine that you are watching a television play with such complete fascination that you become totally identified with one of the characters. And then you become that character. You forget that there is this other self sitting in the chair in the living room and watching the screen. When the drama ends, perhaps, you will wake up and go back to your consciousness in the chair.

Take another image. Think of a man fishing in a stream. The bait is the ego, and the fish is the experience the daimon wishes to draw toward itself. The fisherman looking down through the water is the daimon looking down through all the vibratory *lokas* of space-time at the ego caught by hook and line into certain karmic, historical circumstances. If you identify with the ego, it's not a very nice position to be in; but if you identify with the fisherman, then it just might turn out to be a beautiful day by a mountain stream. I suppose if you were to identify with the fingernail as it gets clipped, the experience could be made to be painful. Once again, you can look at the meditational paths of the great religions as attempts to make the ego seem merely the fingernail of the soul. That such a shift in consciousness is so difficult indicates how well Set, or Lucifer, or Tezcatlipoca has done his job. If we were not trapped into the coffin, we would break out immediately and go back to lollygagging with the fairies in the realms of dreams. (Notice how when LSD broke people out of their boxes, they flew instantly back to the astral-plane realm of faeryland.) And so we are nailed down into space-time and have to complete the cycle of evolution before we can reascend, but at that time it is to be hoped that we will take the body on up with us.

The ego is with us for a purpose. If we adopt the ego-annihilation techniques of some sects, we frustrate the mystery of incarnation. The annihilation of the ego is simply the linked, mirror-opposite of the materialism which says only the ego is real. What is called for is a shift in consciousness in which the ego is figured against the ground of the daimon.

To see the ego as figure against the ground of the daimon, we need to experience time in a different way. Mystics speak of "the eternal now," but this phrase is generally interpreted to mean an eternal succession of points, or ticks of the clock, or beats of the heart. "Now" becomes an instant *in* time that will go on repeating itself endlessly. The difficulty with this view is that it sees "now" as a duration, a serial extension, whereas "the eternal now" is really something that is at right angles to the flow of time. The eternal now is not a moment, not an interval of duration; it is the timeless background against which all serial instants of time are figured. It is the space between each heartbeat, the doorway to eternity. Our heart beats a rhythm which locks us into time, but as any contemplative knows, the interval between each heartbeat can be extended so that a timeless space opens to us in which we are no longer in the time frame of the ego and its pressing concerns and desires. We do not have to escape to the Himalayas; we simply have to quiet our thoughts and passions, still the breath and the heartbeat, and move into another kind of space and time, in which the ego is merely part of a much larger whole. If we run about in an excited rage, trying to make money, improve the world, or start a revolution, we simply slam the door of our cage and waste time beating against the bars, screaming to be let out.

The Chinese classic the *Tao Te Ching* has a poem which points out that the usefulness of a cup comes from the empty space, the part of the cup which is not there. Being and nonbeing are bound up in the architecture of something as simple as a cup. So it is with the architecture of the human heart. The interval between the heartbeats is like the empty space of the cup. As the ego fills with the plenitude of the soul, it becomes aware that the body is still seated in meditation, but that body is no longer the center of consciousness. It is as if a new self has come in to observe, from outside the ego's time frame, the time of the personality. In an old book forgotten by philosophers but remembered by writers of science fiction, *An Experiment with Time*, J. W. Dunne presents a model of a serial universe in which there are parallel time streams. If you observe yourself in time, there must be another vantage point in which that observation is being made, and so on in a regress ad infinitum. Dunne's model is mathematical and geometrical, but in its simpler forms it can be used to look at the familiar experience of astral projection.

Children who do not know that they are not allowed to have experiences of floating out of their bodies will sometimes come to their parents and ask what it means when, before they wake up in the bed in the morning, they see themselves down in the bed, but they are floating up near the ceiling. Many parents would dismiss their children's experience as a mere dream (without having a clue as to what *dreams* are all about) and tell them to forget about such things. No doubt these parents have a fear that such a twinning of the self might mean that their child is schizophrenic, and so they try to push the child into normalcy, and thereby increase the chances of a serious splitting later on. Other parents will know about the out-of-the-body experience and can simply take down a book from the shelf, show the child a drawing by a person who has had a similar experience, and treat the whole thing as nothing to be disturbed about. If you live in a culture in which these experiences are understood, then the experiences can go on *in* culture; therefore, the individual is rescued from being *pushed* out of his mind by a so-called "normal" society.

Now when you see yourself down in the bed but you are floating over the body in the air, what is the nature of the flow of time in one body and the other? The Sufi guru Pir Vilayat Khan says that there is another stage when this second body goes to sleep and a third body, the causal body, awakens and moves up to a much higher level of vibration, and so we must assume that the time-space frame will change again. There seem to be separate but parallel time-space flows for the physical, astral, and causal bodies. Perhaps we shouldn't call them "bodies"; perhaps, with a mind to Whitehead's criticism of the doctrine of "simple location," we should think of them as envelopes of energy with differing space-time properties as the attention of the being is directed into one form or another. When the attention of the psyche is in one form, we feel ourselves to be in that body, be it physical, astral, or causal. When we are thinking in the habits of the ego, we tend to think of the body as the extent of ourselves, limited in three dimensions. Ironically, we wouldn't think of an elementary particle in that way; and since the body is far more complex than an elementary particle, it would seem appropriate to view it as a multidimensional field of energy with different time-space properties.

According to the Indian Upanishads, every night in dreamless sleep the soul returns to the feet of Brahman. Dreamless sleep is the samadhi state; the brain-wave patterns for a yogi in samadhi and a normal person in dreamless sleep are the same. The great exception is that the yogi can watch his mind go from waking to sleep to dreamless sleep, whereas for the rest of us this extension of consciousness is not yet possible. If in dreamless sleep the soul goes back to the feet of Brahman, then the diurnal cycle is a microcosm of the macrocosmic cycle of creation and return to God. The soul is a hologram which mirrors the entirety of creation within itself. We can look out at the world through physics, or we can look inward through mysticism, but the world is one and not two.

Now let's look inward for a moment to go back to the experiences of dreams and astral projection. A common memory of astral projection is the dream of flying; but in these dreams there are two distinct experiences of flight. In one the body is buoyant and floating, but always returning to earth; in the other the body is soaring. Now according to Pir Vilayat Khan, the experience of the denser body floating is an experience of the etheric body, or what the Theosophists call the subtle-physical body. The experience of soaring at great heights is an experience of the astral body. A guru, such as Pir Vilayat, can go beyond the astral with the causal body through the practice of *yoga nidra*, the yoga of sleep; and a paramahamsa can go beyond the karmic world of the causal plane into the unmanifest, the world of pure bliss, the world of *satchitananda*. The great soul remembers the diurnal rhythm of waking, sleeping, dreaming, and returning to the feet of Brahman; the rest of us forget. We move unconsciously from dreamless sleep to the astral world, and then hover over our physical body in our etheric bodies, dreaming dreams that are the memories of the experiences we have had; and then we wake up, remembering the dreams which are the memories of the experiences in other dimensions. And so it is all like a Chinese box within a box within a box.

To map out these boxes within boxes with the help of Dunne's model of the serial universe, let us imagine the physical body as dense and heavy, a long wavelength, a lower vibration; then let us imagine that the movement from one body to another is a movement to a shorter and higher wavelength with a different flow of time and space. The model would then look something like the figure. In the

model for the sake of symbolism the vibrations are shown increasing in a geometric progression until finally they become so high that they disappear, and the line of satchitananda expresses the condition in which all the vibrations have gone beyond into nondifferentiation, pure void, *sunyata*.

At this point, since I'm in way over my head, I would like to make a theological guess. I would like to play the role of Christian theologian to imagine that the flat, undifferentiated line bends round again, like a yin-yang symbol, and becomes matter, the physical universe. The physical, supposedly the densest and most removed from the higher vibrations of the divine, becomes recognized for what it is, "the Mystical Body of Christ." Both Sri Aurobindo and Teilhard de Chardin speak of the process of evolution as the "divinization of matter," and both are, therefore, intent on avoiding any Gnostic transcendentalism which denies the divinity of the physical universe. So I prefer to imagine that black holes expand the light of dying stars into other dimensions, and that "the end of all our exploring," in the words of T. S. Eliot, "will be to arrive where we started and know the place for the first time."[1]

Now as you consider each of the wavelengths of the various bodies in the figure, it would seem that a different flow of time is expressed for each one. If you are floating over your body and about to go off on various experiences, what may seem like a long time to you may be only taking up a moment, an interval in the rapid eye movements of the physical body. Just such a model of time occurs in fairy tales and is repeated by C. S. Lewis in his Chronicles of Narnia. When the children go through the wardrobe into Narnia, they never know how much time has gone by in the ordinary world. According to the theory of relativity an astronaut returning from another galaxy would come home to find that centuries had elapsed on earth since his departure. He would experience the fate of the ancient voyager Bran, who returned to Ireland to find that his men turned to dust as if they were centuries old as soon as they set foot on land. As he inquired of the time of the people on the shore, Bran found that "The Voyage of Bran" was one of their most ancient legends, and he turned away from death in Ireland to go off for unknown wanderings. So the box within a box quality of time confronts us in ancient literature as well as in modern science fiction.

The traditional way of expressing the difference in the time of the ego and the time of the daimon is through the images of the line and the circle. The line expresses the time of the ego, a linear extension through a series of repeating units; the circle expresses a fullness in which consciousness is everywhere present at once. The pre-Socratic philosopher Empedocles described God (in words that seem as well to fit Yeats's description of the daimon): "For He is equal in all directions unto Himself, a rounded sphere enjoying a circular solitude." When you are simply located in your ego, you experience extension and duration, but when consciousness is drawn into the vanishing point in meditation, it expands to infinity in a new dimension. The world of the ego is a geometry of points, distances, and separations; but as you move out through the doorway between each heartbeat, the space becomes one in which "the center is everywhere, and the circumference nowhere."

If the daimon is a rounded sphere enjoying a circular solitude, then it need not do anything or go anywhere, for all knowledge would be mirrored in the cosmic hologram of its own unity. Now the central mystery of the Fall is that we must somehow assume that this unlimited state is limited. Set traps Osiris for a reason; Quetzalcoatl is shown his body by the deceiving Tezcatlipoca; Eve is tricked by Lucifer. The Fall into the body breaks up the old steady-state of the universe and permits a new creative disequilibrium to shock evolution into a new direction. Why? No one can say, but the myths indicate that an easy, blissed-out unity is not the ultimate answer to the riddle of existence. The soul's imperative is not to escape history but to absorb it and transmute it. The project of the soul is not to annihilate the ego but to allow the soul to use the ego as the ego uses the hand. Out of the innumerable incarnations of many separate egos comes the possibility for communication on an even higher level. For Western man, history, rather than being *maya* or illusion, is the embodiment of an unfathomable mystery. This is what esoteric Christianity is all about.

The ego is the line, the daimon is the circle, but the archetypal image of the resolution of the line and the circle is the spiral, for the spiral is the basic image of dynamic growth. Whether it is a seashell, a nebula, or the widening gyres in the poetry of Yeats, the spiral expresses a movement that includes as it unfolds. In this movement history appears to include old ages in its unfoldment into new ones. In the eyes of such metahistorians as Yeats, Hegel, or Giambattista Vico, history turns and raises into consciousness the old as it moves away from it in the new. Vico saw these spirals of time as a *"corso, ricorso"* of four basic ages; but the theory of history we call Viconian, is not really his own but a borrowing from the ancient Egyptians.

For the ancient Egyptians there were four great ages to the life of a civilization: the ages of Gods, of Heroes, of Men, and of Chaos. Each of these four ages has a corresponding form of language. The Age of Gods has hieroglyphic language; the Age of Heroes has aristocratic language; the Age of Men has the commercial language of the marketplace; and the Age of Chaos has the degeneration of language into mere jargon and cant. Hieroglyphic language would be like the sacred cosmic language of the ancient Egyptians or of the Maya of Central America. Aristocratic language would be the elegant speech of the courtier, a Castiglione or a Sir Philip Sidney. The language of the Age of Men is the language we have had with us since the Industrial Revolution, and now that we are entering the Age of Chaos, language has decayed into the jargon of the social sciences and the grunts of the drug culture. In hieroglyphic language, every thought, no matter how abstract, is related to a concrete visual image or a root form of the word, as in Sanskrit, but in the language of Chaos, mind is disconnected from body, and concepts are disconnected from experience, and so words like "pacification" are used for bombing and "relocation" for imprisonment in concentration camps. When President Nixon's press secretary had to admit that an earlier statement of his was a lie, he used the language of the Age of Chaos and said, "That statement is no longer operative."

Now if we take this model of the four ages and apply it to historical time, we can begin to see a *rough* correspondence. "History begins at Sumer," and so we begin with the Age of the Gods in the urban revolution around 3500 B.C. The Sumerians themselves insisted that they did not build the cities but that the gods did: before man moved into the cities they were inhabited by the gods. In the early days of Sumerian culture, the ruler of a city was called a steward, an *ensi;* he administered the city for the absentee landlord, the god, who would return some day. As time went by, people forgot about the god who was supposed to return, and secular politics took over from sacred trusteeship. The steward evolved into a king. The Age of Gods was over and the Age of Heroes had begun. It is at this point that we get those historical figures, such as Sargon of Agade, who set up monuments in honor of their conquests. Once the process of secularization, war, conquest, and internal political strife is set in motion, there is no stopping, and history becomes a list of changing dynasties. The Age of Heroes recedes and petty king succeeds petty king through the Age of Men. At long last the culture reaches the point where it has become so corrupt that it no longer believes in anything, not gods, heroes, or men. The Age of Chaos comes, and the internal rot enables the nomadic tribes to invade the cities and great Ur is given over to the wind. Or perhaps we should think that the desert wind is the body of the god returned to live in the city and sweep all the little men out.

One of the men who could hear the voice in the whirlwind was Abraham, and it is Abraham's people, or, at least, one branch of them, who are credited by some scholars with the destruction of Ur at the beginning of the second millennium B.C. With Father Abraham, the spiral turns and we go back to the Age of the Gods in a Viconian *ricorso*. From 4000 to 2000 we have the Platonic magnus annus of two thousand years, the season of time in which it takes Sumerian civilization to run from the Age of Gods to the Age of Chaos. At 2000 B.C. a new cycle begins, and the primitive nomadic culture of the Hebrews begins its descent toward the Age of Chaos. At the beginning of the cycle it is still very much the Age of Gods, for Father Abraham can walk and talk to Jahweh directly. Jahweh promises Abraham that his seed will be as numberless as the stars of the sky and the sand of the desert, but Father Abraham is a practical, down-to-earth trader, and so he asks, "How shall I know this, Lord?" Somehow the man of caravans is able to talk Jahweh into signing a contract and putting it in writing, for the covenant is simply that, a contract. In the Age of Gods the most abstract and cosmic ideas are concrete. The great divorce between sacred and profane, mind and body, comes later with the process of class stratification, secularization, and demythologizing. Abraham, the beloved of God, is still the crafty trader who knows how to drive a bargain even with the Almighty.

But this closeness and familiarity with God only lasts for the season of the Age of Gods. By the time we come to the Age of Heroes with Moses, we have not the prosaic man of caravans but the stern hero standing on top the volcanic mountain and bearing the tablets of the Law. But for all his heroic stature, Moses cannot look Jahweh in the face or walk out to converse with him. Jahweh is veiled, and when he reveals even his backside to Moses, he must place him in the crevice of a rock lest he be hurled and smashed against the mountain. The movement through the four ages is like the decay of a radioactive substance with a specific half-life; each age receives half of the divine power and charisma of the former era. As we move forward through time, it may look like power, glory, and the increase of the GNP to the depraved, but the wise know just how much of the true power of the culture has been lost.

When we move from Moses and the Age of Heroes to the Age of Men, we come to greedy little people such as Ahab and Jezebel, who are concerned with "making it" on the civilized and affluent terms of the Canaanites. A prophet such as Elijah is a terrifying figure who can put the prophets of Baal to the sword in a *herrem,* the Hebrew equivalent of a jihad, but Elijah is not Moses. He cannot create a new moral nation or awaken the people to remember the days of Abraham, Isaac, and Jacob. His is a holding action against the inevitable movement toward the Age of Chaos.

And the Age of Chaos did come. The temple of Jerusalem is destroyed and the Jews are taken into captivity. From the Babylonian Captivity to the second destruction of the Temple by the Romans in A.D. 70 is the Age of Chaos of Hebrew civilization. But chaos from the mythopoeic point of view provides the fertile decay needed to generate a new civilization. The Ouroboros bites its tail to release the poison needed for its own regeneration; the phoenix rises on his own ashes into the sky. In the *Vision* of Yeats, it is when the dark gyre is at its widest that the tiny point of light of the new gyre begins to rotate in the opposite direction.

And so, *corso, ricorso,* the cycle turns, and Jesus is born in the blackest part of the Age of Chaos. For our Western European civilization, Jesus is the avatar, the annunciator of the new Age of the Gods. Now one of the interesting things about the Age of Gods is that it is invisible to all except those who are attuned and receptive to the gods. All that the rest of the world can see is the continuation of the Age of Chaos. It is as if a star were born in the heavens, but its normal light would take years before it can be seen in the sky, and so when normal people look up to the sky, they see the past, but those who have been caught up in a high contemplation of the music of the spheres have heard the good news or have seen a more than usual movement of angels from on high.

Jesus begins the new magnus annus, the new two-thousand-year cycle. The Gospels tell of his public life, but the esoteric legends go further in imagination to speak about Jesus's wanderings to the ancient temples. One legend tells of Jesus going to Glastonbury with his uncle, Joseph of Arimathea, and there on a shrine of enormous antiquity, the new age is kindled. It is to Glastonbury that King Arthur will come to create the kingdom destined to grow into a worldwide empire.

King Arthur marks the beginning of the Age of Heroes; for the culture of the English-speaking people, Arthur is the dominant archetypal hero. Knights and kings come and go through Christendom, but the image of King Arthur and his knights of the round table never loses its fascination. But by the time of the Renaissance, the image is beginning to recede into the world of literature only. Spenser gives an antiquerian's polish to chivalry, but the world is turning away from heroes and knights, and, therefore, paying them their last respects in the works of Spenser, Ariosto, and Cervantes. The new Age of Men is dawning, and it is an age in which a foot soldier with a firearm can bring a shining knight in armor down to the dirt. The world of lands held in fealty is

changing into capitalism and the rise of a new world economy. The civil servant and the accountant will begin to be
more important in the consolidation of the nation-state than
a convocation of proud and independent knights.

The Age of Men is the age of military dictators such as
Cromwell or corrupt prime ministers such as Castlereagh.
The climax of the Age of Men comes with the Industrial
Revolution, when the black-suited capitalists from Man-
chester and Birmingham range over all the world. From
Manchester to Pittsburgh to Detroit to Los Angeles to
Tokyo and Osaka, the businessmen have gone out, turning
forests into Kleenex, blue skies into smog, oceans into cess-
pools, and governments into teams of economists. With
these latter days of the Industrial Revolution, the Age of
Chaos is at hand.

And so the cycle spins round again, and the two-
thousand-year magnus annus of Jesus draws to its tumultu-
ous close. War, famine, weather changes, terrorism, and the
complete moral collapse of anything resembling human culture in such places as Northern Ireland and Lebanon begin
to tell us what the modern world is coming to. And now we
wait and wonder whether economic collapse, ecological catastrophe, and thermonuclear war are all that remain to be
played out in the declining years of the second millennium A.D.

But once again the myth holds true and the Age of Chaos
is providing the fertile decay for the regeneration of the Age
of Gods. We are turning on the spiral of history and going
through the difficult times of Abraham and Jesus, but out of
the disintegration of postindustrial civilization is emerging
an entirely new sacred world culture. Now don't rush out
into the streets to try to see Jesus landing in a flying saucer,
for that is simply the ego looking for a cheap religious thrill.
I doubt if any of us will live to see the full implications of

anything that I am talking about. Civilizations change in the twinkling of an eye, but it takes centuries for those changes to become visible to the masses. Events like the neolithic revolution or the Renaissance do occur, but they don't take place within the time frame of the individual ego. The normal people who were alive at the time of Jesus would not have noticed anything: life would still be measured out in the sale of so many jars of olive oil; but for all that, a new civilization was born. And so it is now.

There is one way, however, in which massive transformations become visible, and that is through the process of unconscious miniaturization. When the hominids left the forest millions of years ago, the forests became miniaturized in the clump of trees in the open savanna where the females and the infants stayed while the males ranged out to hunt for food. When humans left hunting, then the animals became miniaturized in domestication, and neolithic man no longer had to range out to hunt for food. When humans left the country for the city, then the country became miniaturized in a garden. When humanity left Christendom behind for commercial civilization in the Industrial Revolution, then Christendom became miniaturized in Augustus Pugin's Medieval Court in the Great Exhibition of 1851. And now that humanity is leaving urban civilization behind, civilization is becoming miniaturized in the architecture of Paolo Soleri's "arcologies." If humanity leaves the planet, then the planet will become miniaturized in one of Professor Gerard O'Neill's space colonies. O'Neill's space colonies express the exoteric and technological process of miniaturization, but a more esoteric process is expressed in the philosophy of Sri Aurobindo.

When humans evolve beyond the mental level into "the supramental level of consciousness," then, I believe, the mental world will become miniaturized. In many ways this transformation has already begun. As the culture begins to make the shift from the mental to the supramental level, the old mental level is becoming miniaturized and turned into a work of art. Since McLuhan has called the artists the early-warning system of cultural change, you can observe this shift in levels of consciousness in the work of the artists, not the official ones in the galleries and literary salons who go around carrying signs saying "*I* am an artist!" but the less obvious and pretentious expressions of imagination. Since official art has become, in this Age of Chaos, a public relations business, art has been reduced to tricks, gimmicky fads, and sycophantism. Each culture gets the art it deserves, and so the artist, like a boil on the skin, simply tells us that we are sick. But art not only records the present, it helps to create the future. Art is also an agent of transformation.

To see the transformation, you have to think big, and, therefore, this kind of art is mythopoeic rather than abstract or mimetic. The expression of myth, cosmology, and the sacred, not to mention the aesthetic, has moved into more honest and direct expressions such as nonfiction. Think of the nonfiction of Lewis Thomas or Carlos Castaneda. In my own works *At the Edge of History* and *Passages About Earth*, I was attempting to build a form that had the structure of art but the content of scholarship. The cultural responses to poem and novel had become so studied and mannered under the corporate management of the literature departments that there was little room left to challenge the cultural description of reality itself. Everyone knows a poem is mere subjective feeling, and everyone knows a novel is not true, but I was more concerned with the horizon where fact and feeling, myth and reality came together. What was true of my own experiments is even truer of the work of Castaneda and Thomas.

Just as it takes three points to draw a curve, it took three writers for me to connect the points and see a cultural pattern. The art of the Age of Chaos was complex, tricky, and avant-garde; it was custom-made for the consumerism of the latter days of capitalism. The art of the new Age of the Gods was simple, direct, and mythopoeic; it was a performance of reality and not a description. In music, it was Karlheinz Stockhausen's *Stimmung*, a litany of the names of the gods of history in which the music was not a horizontal progression of harmonies, but a vertical space of timbre. The single chord chanted for seventy minutes becomes with each sound, a mandala, a hieroglyph. With *Stimmung*, Stockhausen put all the precious and arty pretentiousness of his early "avant-garde" work behind him; he moved from creating music of the twentieth-century, the Age of Chaos, to creating the new music of the Age of the Gods.

Most artists do not like this talks of gods, for they have grown up on a fashionable cynicism which makes their own egos the most important part of the universe. Remarks I have made before on art have made many artists angry, for in our secular world art is the only religion that is taken seriously. You can look up at the sky on a clear summer's night in the Hamptons and tell an artist, "God is dead," and he will drink to that; but if you survey his world of Manhattan and East Hampton and tell him, "Art is dead," he will be scandalized, for that is really blasphemy.

For people caught up in the alienation of the modern corporate world, art is all that is left to live by. The need to be creative, to feel sophisticated, to belong to the world of success has created a market for art. If the directors of the Marlborough Gallery thought that art was dead, they would go out and pay people to fill their galleries with anything that would keep the rich and the famous coming back. Since it would not be difficult to find people who would be willing to stuff the galleries so that they too could become rich and famous, we can assume that art would go on long after it was dead. In fact, just such an imaginary situation has been going on for some time.

From another point of view, of course, it is pointless to attack the decay of art or the decay of an entire civilization. Decay is part of life; the Age of Chaos and not the Age of Heroes is the prelude to the new Age of the Gods. The best way to attune to the new age is not to criticize the old but to move beyond it.

When the work of the intellect becomes a mind dance, the performance of intellection shifts from separation, analysis, and control to expression, synthesis, and co-operation. The play of the intellect begins to be one of expressive connectiveness and not analytical dissections: *Wissenkunst* and not *Wissenschaft*. And now, I hope that it is obvious what I have been up to in these four talks. If you have been trying to digest each idea as it came, you have probably gotten mad at me as I've moved from one idea to another. In other lectures I have had people shout at me to stop or to go more slowly, but that kind of disorientation anxiety comes from staying in one rut, instead of flying over the landscape to see the configuration of patterns. Think of the ancient Irish art of manuscript illumination in the Book of Kells or the Lindisfarne Gospels: overload and abundance is part of the pattern; the pages teem with little beasties curling around every letter; every word threatens to become a hieroglyph, every page a sensuous embodiment of knowledge. The oral presentation of ideas can have its own similar overflowing movement, as long as you sit back and take the flow of words as a shower and not a meal to be digested. The play of a talk, as opposed to the work of an academic lecture, is to suggest, to connect, to juggle with ideas, to play the fool.

To persist in my folly, I would say that in our immediate

Age of Chaos, separation, analysis, and control will continue until the specialized experts inflict upon themselves a kind of professional aphasia in which no generalizations are possible. Knowledge, in reaching its widest dissemination through mass education, will achieve the maximum distribution of energy that we know as entropy; and high culture, science, art, and philosophy will simply come to a halt. The expert will persist in his specialty to become an ignoramus, but the fool, following Blake, will persist in his folly to become wise.

But as knowledge moves toward disintegration at one level of order, it will achieve integration at a higher level: the rocket that creates all hell beneath itself is headed for the sky. The Age of Chaos is giving birth to a new Age of the Gods, and so the future of knowledge will be a return to hieroglyphic thought. We will not simply go back to Egypt or Yucatan; we will go forward to a remythologizing and resacralization in which science, art, and religion will converge in a new cosmic language for initiates. This resacralization, will involve a shift from centering our awareness in the ego to figuring it against the ground of the daimon. In the future, daimonic levels of thought will be more a normal part of daily life rather than the isolated instants of mystical experience that they tend to be now.

What will daimonic thought be like? I imagine it will be like a four-voice fugue, and I would go back to Plato's fourfold model to attempt an approximation of hieroglyphic thought. The persistence of the fourfold vision through history, from Plato to Dante, Vico, Blake, Marx, Yeats, and McLuhan, is itself an indication that fourfold structures are probably related to an archetype at the level of knowledge of the daimon or "the causal plane." The physicist speaks of the four basic forces, and the biologist speaks of the four nucleotides that make up the code of information in our cells. Vico speaks of the four ages, and Yeats of the four faculties. In keeping with this archetypal level of symmetry, I would propose that there are four levels to hieroglyphic thinking:

1. A melodic line
2. A geometrical figure
3. An equation
4. An archetypal image

The first level of hieroglyphic thought is the melodic line. The sound goes forth from God, and the universe is created in the enunciation of the AUM. As the music plays itself out in all the variations of the hidden names of God, it begins to freeze into the crystalline forms of thought to become a geometrical figure. This figure is the seed-form or archetype of the spatial properties that will dominate the universe of matter to come. Architecture has been described as frozen music, and the geometrical figure should be seen as the reconstitution of the nature of the melodic line in physical space. As the geometrical figure dances itself into being, it expresses certain kinds of relationships and symmetries, and these can be reconstituted in an equation. This kind of relationship between equation and geometrical figure is explored in the field of topology, especially in the recent work of the "catastrophe theory" of the French mathematician René Thom. According to Pythagoras, "The All is number," and the equation expresses the numerical properties of the emergent universe. Finally, all of the three levels are expressed in an existential image, an archetype, and the archetype is simply a compressed myth.

Now you should not think of these four levels as a serial progression; like the voices in a fugue, they are all going on at once. For purposes of explanation, I have separated them, but in the consciousness of the daimon they are simulta-

neous plays of energy as eternal delight. Of course, to understand all of this, one would have to be an advanced yogi,
a musician, a geometer, a mathematician, a physicist, and a
poet. The knowledge is dizzyingly complex and far beyond
the capacity of an individual ego; but ultimately it all becomes simple again in the form of the archetypal image as a
compressed myth or child's fairy tale. You can talk about the
solar wind and the deflection of the proton bombardment by
the earth's magnetic field, give an equation for it and show
the shape of the solar wind's interaction with the earth; or
you can say that Father Sun shoots arrows at Mother Earth,
but Mother Earth holds up a shield to knock the arrows
away. You can remark from spatial exploration that the
lightning on the planet Jupiter extends to its moons, or you
can say in myth that Zeus is the great god who hurls enormous lightning bolts.

"The end of all our exploring will be to arrive where we
started and know the place for the first time."[2] And so we
become as little children, and our myths, legends, and fairy
tales tell us stories about the great life of the universe. This
concentricity of sacred knowledge has been attempted before in other cultures, such as that of ancient Egypt or Mexico, but even in our own Western civilization there have
been great constructions of thought that have had the char-
acteristics of hieroglyphic modes of expression. In the early
music of the Middle Ages and the Renaissance, the works of
Machaut and Dunstable are filled with mathematical allu-
sions. From one point of view, the structures are highly
complex, but from another point of view, the music is simple and sensuously beautiful. The cathedral of Chartres is
a celebration of mathematics, but in its sculptures it is also a
story, or *the* story of the Bible.

We are, I believe, in the early stages of constructing a
grand edifice of thought and spirit. What the future cathe-

dral of Chartres will be, I have no way of knowing, but I imagine someone playing a musical instrument and expressing with it certain images in algebra and topology; as the instrument is played, the physical form of the building is created. Perhaps my fantasy is simply one of a Bach-like God sitting at the keyboard of the universe, but I imagine a future architecture in which you turn on a building the way we now turn on the lights. These buildings will be temporary like concerts, and not enduring like the pyramids; and so when the use of the building is finished, the people can move on. The culture will be similar to the nomadic way of life of the old paleolithic hunters and gatherers; the people will carry their cultures in their souls, and so familiar will they be with earth, wind, and stars that civilization will be unnecessary. Perhaps, rather than imagining the future, I am merely seeing the past. Perhaps even before Atlantis the hunters and gatherers of the past were not savages but initiates of cosmic mysteries. Past or future, it does not matter, for the distant future will see a return of the remote past.

The archetypes of melody, figure, equation, and mythic image are like seed crystals from the causal plane; as they are dropped into time, they take time to exfoliate all their compressed possibilities. And so if you are thinking on the daimonic level, you will see or feel things that are there all at once but that will take ages of historical time to unfold. This is why prophets should not try to make predictions; they too often become confused at the relationship of what they are seeing in visions to the actual playing out of these visions in history. Before I had *darshan* with the Mother of the Sri Aurobindo Ashram in Pondicherry, India, I was told that the Mother, then in her nineties, was at work on the cells of her body to reverse the aging process. The Mother had obviously seen something concerning the relationship of consciousness and the body in the future, and had spoken of it to her disciples. But ultimately her visions only confused her followers, for they expected her not to die but to manifest a divine child in a supramental body through the return of Sri Aurobindo. The Mother with the divine child is timeless myth, older by far than Christianity; such a supramental embodiment would literally express the ending of time. And so the followers were disappointed and could not understand it when the Mother died.

We are all living at the overture to a new magnus annus, and if we listen in meditation, we can hear music from the future playing variations on themes from the past. But it will take two thousand years to play out all the themes suggested by the overture. If we center in our egos and scream in the words of the chorus in *Marat/Sade,* "We want our revolution NOW," we become like infants screaming for a bottle, or crying for Christmas to come early. If we shift out of the demands of the ego into the contemplative spaces of meditation, then we can see, in the fullness of a "hyperspace" in which the center is everywhere, that the future is already here and now. That fullness, however, requires the rich addition of the concrete embodiment of this specific moment in history. The ego is to the daimon as the musical instrument is to the virtuoso: he does not smash it in a fit of rage because the notes come only one at a time; he plays with it lovingly to let the music suggest the mysteries of time; the fugue is complete only when it is finished and no longer there.

In these talks on the future I have not tried to play the prophet and predict the shape of things to come. I have used imagination to expand upon the implications of the present; for everything I am talking about is already here, from the new Age of the Gods to the return of hieroglyphic thought. Hieroglyphic thought is expressed in the old cathedrals and the ancient pyramids, but we are also trying to express it at Lindisfarne, for Lindisfarne, in name and action, is the embodiment of a myth. The monks at the first Lindisfarne in seventh-century Northumbria did not live to see Oxford University or the great cathedrals of England coming out of their work, and the latter-day monks of the present Lindisfarne will not live to see people who can express all the four levels of hieroglyphic thinking. Nevertheless, I believe that after the feeble experiments of our Lindisfarne are finished, there will come a school with a new kind of medieval quadrivium, a curriculum in which music, geometry, sacred architecture, mathematics, language, and mythological poetry will be the vision of an education in a culture beyond anything our technological civilization dreams about in its lust for the "conquest" of space.

But before we can experience this level of the daimon, we will have to experience the defeat of the ego. We have declared war on the ecosystem with industry, and war on evolution with genetic engineering, and we will have to endure the defeats our own arrogance will inflict upon us. No one knows the future, but I would guess that we will have to be turned upside down and emptied before we can be stood upright and filled.

AFTERWORD

THESE FOUR TALKS on the future were given in October of 1976 on the occasion of the opening of the Lindisfarne Association in New York City. Lindisfarne began in 1973 in Southampton, New York, as a more or less rural contemplative community of students devoted to the study and realization of a new planetary culture, but the increasingly global extent of our concerns for contemporary culture soon found us moving into the world city of New York. In the country the community had struggled to envision and create an alternative future; in the city the community now struggles to work toward that future in the middle of an overpowering and often depressing contemporary urban society.

Since its founding in 1973, Lindisfarne has grown from a handful of teachers and students in Southampton to an association of religious thinkers, scientists, artists, and scholars all around the world who are working to effect a cultural transformation of humanity. From the New Alchemy Institute in Massachusetts to the Intermediate Technology Group in England, the Findhorn Community in Scotland, the Research Foundation for Eastern Wisdom and Western Science in Germany, the Sri Aurobindo Ashram in Pondicherry, India, and Zen Center in California, the members of the Lindisfarne Association are at work together in a cultural movement as ambitious as the Renaissance.

The people of the Lindisfarne community believe that humanity is in a period of profound evolutionary change and that the earth itself is undergoing changes with us. These changes are now expressing themselves negatively as global pollution and ecological disruption, but these signs of destruction can also be read to indicate that the old relationship between nature and culture is breaking up and that out of this creative disequilibrium a new adaptation of consciousness and matter is emerging.

Mechanists see this transformation as one in which nature becomes contained by man to become little more than a potted plant in a space colony. The members of the Lindisfarne Association, however, see this transformation as one in which technological civilization becomes miniaturized and surrounded by a consciousness no longer polarized between mind and body, conscious and unconscious, male and female, spirit and matter. The mechanist seeks to control and dominate nature, and this lack of compassion for all sentient beings leads to a technological elitism which seeks to control and dominate all societies. But when the scientist works with a sense of the sacredness of all existence, he moves into a higher consciousness shared with the artist and the mystic.

To recover a sense of the sacred in science, it is often necessary to go back to preindustrial forms of knowledge. Whether we speak of New Alchemy, Taoist science, or Pythagorean science, the scholars of Lindisfarne are referring to a paradigm shift in Western science in which art, religion, and science reconverge in a new way of knowing and being in the universe.

The recovery of the sense of the sacred in all forms of

human culture is the unity behind all of the activities of Lindisfarne. Whether we are working at a seminar or in the kitchen, we seek to uncover that consciousness in which the individual is uplifted by the immensity of the divine life embodied in the unique moment of his own existence; therefore, meditation is at the heart of the life of the community and at the foundation of any particular course of study.

As an association of individuals and groups around the world, Lindisfarne is working with others toward the following common goals:

1. The spiritual transformation of individual consciousness.
2. The realization of the esoteric unity of all the great universal religions.
3. The fostering of a new harmony between nature and culture through the creation of new metaindustrial villages and smaller, decontralized, symbiotic cities.
4. The expression of a sympathetic resonance among all the richly diverse cultures of human evolution through the creation of a world polity beyond the present materialistic civilization of warring industrial nation-states and exploited preindustrial societies.

NOTES

ONE

1. A. F. C. Wallace, "Revitalization Movements," *American Anthropologist*, LVIII (April 1956), pp. 264–81.

2. Glyn Daniel, *The Idea of Prehistory* (Cleveland: World, 1962), p. 32. See also H. R. Hays, *From Ape to Angel:* An Informal History of Social Anthropology (New York: Capricorn, 1964), p. x.

3. William Irwin Thompson, *The Imagination of an Insurrection: Dublin, Easter 1916* (New York: Oxford, 1967), p. 30.

4. Erich Kahler, *The Tower and the Abyss* (New York: Braziller, 1957).

5. Pierre Teilhard de Chardin, *The Future of Man* (New York: Harper & Row, 1964), pp. 130, 132.

6. Immanuel Wallerstein, *The Modern World System: The Origins of Capitalist Agriculture in the Sixteenth Century* (New York: Academic Press, 1974).

7. Herman Kahn, "From Present to Future: The Problems of Transition to a Postindustrial Society," *Co-Evolution Quarterly*, Fall 1976, pp. 4–17.

8. David Spangler, *Revelation: The Birth of a New Age* (San Francisco: Rainbow Bridge, 1976).

9. *The Findhorn Garden*, (Harper & Row, New York, 1975).

10. Lewis Thomas, "At the Mercy of Our Defenses," in *Earth's Answer: Explorations of Planetary Culture at the Lindisfarne Conferences* (New York: Lindisfarne / Harper & Row, 1977).

11. Lewis Thomas, *The Lives of a Cell* (New York: Viking, 1975).

TWO

1. Howard T. Odum, *Environment, Power, and Society* (New York: Wiley, 1971).

2. Rudolph Steiner, *Cosmic Memory* (West Nyack, N.Y.: Steiner Publications, 1959).

3. Piotr Kropotkin, *Fields, Factories, and Workshops* (New York: Benjamin Blom, 1968).

4. Edward and Faith Andrews, *Shaker Furniture* (New York, Dover, 1964), p. 12.

5. Richard J. Barnett and Ronald E. Müller, *Global Reach: The Power of the Multinational Corporations* (New York: Simon & Schuster, 1974), p. 338.

6. See Russell Schweickart in *Earth's Answer*.

7. See George Cabot Lodge, *The New American Ideology* (New York: Knopf, 1976), p. 125.

8. Elise Boulding, *The Underside of History: A View of Women Through Time* (Boulder, Colo.: Westview Press, 1976), p. 14.

9. See Satprem, *Sri Aurobindo, or the Adventure of Consciousness* (New York: Harper & Row, 1974).

10. See J. Baldwin, "The New Alchemists," in *Co-Evolution Quarterly*, Winter 1976–77, pp. 104–11.

11. Sean Wellesley-Miller and Day Charoudhi, "BioShelter," in *Architecture Plus*, Nov./Dec., 1974.

12. See John Michell, *The Earth Spirit* (London: Thames & Hudson, 1975), p. 15.

13. Lyn Margolis and James E. Lovelock, "The Gaia Hypothesis," *Co-Evolution Quarterly*, Summer 1975, pp. 30–40.
14. Eric Hobsbawm, *The Age of Revolution: 1789–1848* (New York: Signet, 1962), p. 310.

THREE

1. *The Letters of W. B. Yeats*, ed. Allan Wade (London: Rupert-Hart-Davis, 1954), p. 922.
2. L. S. Stavrianos, *The Promise of the Coming Dark Age* (San Francisco: Freeman, 1976).
3. Edward O. Wilson, *Sociobiology: The New Synthesis* (Cambridge: Harvard University Press, 1975), p. 474.
4. Paul D. McLean, M.D., "Man and His Animal Brains," *Modern Medicine*, Feb. 1964, pp. 95–106.
5. Laurette Séjourné, *Burning Water: Thought and Religion in Ancient Mexico* (Berkeley, Calif.: Shambhala, 1976), p. 86.
6. Lyn Margolis and James E. Lovelock, "The Gaia Hypothesis," *Co-Evolution Quarterly*, Summer 1975, pp. 30–40.
7. See *Glastonbury: A Study in Patterns* (Research into Lost Knowledge, 36 College Court, Hammersmith, London, 1969).
8. Gregory Bateson, *Steps to an Ecology of Mind* (New York: Ballantine, 1972), p. 448.
9. See John Michell, *The View over Atlantis* (London: Sago, 1969).

FOUR

1. From "Little Gidding," *The Collected Poetry of T. S. Eliot* (New York, Harcourt Brace, 1943).
2. Ibid.

ACKNOWLEDGMENTS

I wish to express my gratitude to June Cobb, who prepared a transcription of the four talks from the tapes, and to John Micholl, who read the manuscript and contributed helpful suggestions for improvements.